MAN'S QUEST TO ALIGN HIS PATH
WITH GOD'S PURPOSE

OBEDIENCE
VS
SACRIFICE

DUSTAN CHRISTENSEN

Copyright © 2021 DUSTAN R CHRISTENSEN
All Rights Reserved. Printed in the U.S.A.
Published by Two Penny Publishing
850 E Lime Street #266, Tarpon Springs, Florida 34688

All rights reserved. This book or parts thereof may not be reproduced in any form, stored in any retrieval system, or transmitted in any form by any means—electronic, mechanical, photocopy, recording, or otherwise—without prior written permission of the publisher, except as provided by United States of America copyright law.

For permission requests and ordering information, email the publisher at: info@twopennypublishing.com

Library of Congress Control Number: 2021904098

ISBN: 978-1-950995-25-7
eBook also available

FIRST EDITION

For more information about the author or to book an event appearance or media interview, please contact the author representative at: info@twopennypublishing.com

WHAT READERS SAY

Dustan Christensen pushes me to be a better man. He helps me identify how I can improve myself and encourages me to take steps toward my goals.

Dustan has made mistakes, as we all have, and wants to help men avoid those missteps. The growth that I have personally witnessed in the past ten years has been truly amazing. He is an inspiration to me, and I am honored to call him a friend.

I encourage you to read Obedience vs Sacrifice. It will help you navigate the trips and falls of daily life and show you the value of spending time with God and becoming more like Him.

Darin Kane
Telecommunication Worker

In this book, Dustan Christensen shares relatable and intimate details of himself. His mix of stories and scriptures connect with the reader and help bring them closer to God. Dustan shares his fears openly in this book. He inspires me to make better choices in my life.

Previously, I believed that a successful career would bring fulfillment to my life—it didn't. My sacrifices only made me feel lost and alone. I was watering the "weeds" in my life instead of the good seeds God planted in me. Obedience vs Sacrifice helped me understand that my pride was in my way. I have learned to crawl humbly, walk faithfully, and run towards the Roaring Lion.

Scott M. Katzka, LPC, NCC
SFC, US Army Retired

To my loving wife who saved my life.
You believed in the man God made me to be and
gave me the courage to write these words.

In honor of my brother Tim Lee Peterson.
May you continue to fight victoriously in the armies of heaven.
You will never be forgotten, and I miss you every day!

CONTENTS

Introduction 7

1 //
SACRIFICE
Sacrifice in the World Today 13
Why Success, Yet Never Fulfillment? 31

2 //
OBEDIENCE
Half-Hearted Decisions 49
The True Power of Obedience 65

3 //
MATTERS OF THE HEART
How Do We Bridge the Gap? 85
New Territory, New Blessings, New Battles 101

4 //
THE NARROW PATH TO GOD'S PROVISION
God's Army, God's Glory 117

Notes 131
Acknowledgments 133
About the Author 135

INTRODUCTION

As I begin, I need to throw out some disclaimers and be completely honest. The topics in this book are my opinions, based on what helped me make sense of my life. There is no perfection in this information, other than what comes from the Word itself. Learning the difference between Obedience and Sacrifice has brought love to my life in a way I had not previously known. It showed me what it means to serve others for the right reasons, and—most importantly—has brought me closer to my Heavenly Father and his abundance, strength, and grace.

There will be times throughout these pages that you may be called out. Called out to be a better version of yourself, by changing how you think, lead, and serve. The topic of obedience is very touchy in today's world. With tensions regarding race and gender equality, this word is frequently avoided. That is the very issue, and exactly why I wanted to shed light on this subject. To show men they can have a backbone, they can lead well, and they can have more—by doing it the right way. So, while it seems the world doesn't appreciate obedience unless it is to serve someone else's purpose and gain, I hope through these pages you will find hope that God rewards you more for obedience than sacrifice. I believe this because I have seen it first hand. I pray when you're done reading my story, you will understand how to become obedient to God's purpose, and the blessings that come when you live a life of faithfulness.

A lot of what I will give you is my personal experience on these two words or mindsets that I have been aware of for over ten years. You will see that, even though I was aware, I did not always understand how these two words would change the trajectory of my life. While I am nervous and apprehensive in writing it, this story is not my own; and it gives honor to my Heavenly Father for shaping me and molding me into the man I am today. I pray it finds you right in the middle of yours.

It is my intention that, through my story and the many books I have read, this approach to understanding what these words mean in our lives will hopefully help you relate in ways you may not have seen before. Heck, if I am honest, I did not realize until I started to put thought to paper. In order for you to know where I am coming from, we need to break bread and find out who is writing to you. Since we cannot break bread, here is an overview of who I am. I was born and raised in Westfield, Wisconsin, by an amazing community. Yes, community. There were so many people who helped shape me and love me, and some of them probably don't even know the impact they had on me. Growing up on a dairy farm taught me valuable lessons, but it was not fun at the time. I am only now beginning to understand the true value, many years later. My childhood was great because it was filled with going fishing whenever we wanted, riding snowmobiles, hunting, getting stuck in the mud, and learning how to drive farm equipment. All things most kids, even most adults, don't ever get to do in their lifetimes.

Growing up in a Catholic household was great, and served its purpose to *keep me close to God*. I say keep me close to God, because His plans for me were already arranged before I was born. To some, it seems cliché that God kept me close, but let me help you understand why I believe this. When I was young, I felt I didn't really fit in. I was a good athlete and a good student, but didn't really have many close friends. I always felt there was something else for me. Growing up as my father's best friend, and he mine,

I didn't really feel I was a kid. From the outside looking in, I was going to have a good life. I was a good kid, though my parents might say otherwise. Yet there always seemed to be something missing. God kept me close for a life-changing moment that would be the catalyst for this book, and a life I didn't know existed.

When I was 14, our church partnered with a sister church to go on a retreat to the mountains of Colorado. We were nearly 10,800 ft above sea level in some of the most beautiful countryside I have ever seen. We played games, had bible studies and activities, and met tons of people. Not knowing what my faith really meant nor being aware of God's plan in my life, what happened one morning truly set me on a journey for which I am thankful.

I would see college students running and training every day at camp. I surmised that since I regularly ran at home, why not get up and run. I quickly realized it was not such a great idea. Being a naive young man, I got up and decided to head to the Columbine Memorial erected in honor of the Colorado shootings. The day before, it had affected me to the point I was a crying mess and couldn't understand why; I needed an answer. So early the next morning, I arose, excited to prove I was as good as the people who have been running in the mountains for years. I did not make it 20 yards. I tried again after catching my breath, and then again, and again, and again. After an hour of this painstaking journey, I arrived before sunrise. Now please understand, if you have not previously run at that altitude at any age, your lungs, oxygen levels, and red blood cell count are not normal and take weeks to acclimate, not days.

As I sat on a bench catching my breath, awaiting the sunrise over the majestic mountains, that same feeling I had experienced the night before overcame me. I fell to my knees and started praying, telling God I wanted to know Him more intimately. I wanted a large purpose attached to my life, and I gave Him my whole heart. I wanted that empty feeling—that hole, to be filled. An hour later, the sun rose and my spirit was filled with something indescribable, at least for the remainder of the day. It was on this day God opened my heart to his loving will, and I knew he had a plan for me. Others might not get as abrupt a feeling as I had, but we all know there is something inside us that speaks when we should go, when we should listen, when we should stop, and when we should trust. In the pages that follow, I will show you examples from my life of how God changed me into the man who was able to answer the call when I was 14, and why the attitude behind Obedience vs. Sacrifice really changed my life 20 years later.

Disclaimer

Please understand I am just a normal man, with an amazing wife and beautiful daughter. My struggles are similar to your struggles, yet that feeling God put inside me at the Columbine Memorial finally made sense when I understood the proper relationship of Obedience to Sacrifice. Trust me when I say the last 20 years have incorporated too much sacrifice for the wrong reasons, yet it's the way the world programmed me, and I am sure you, to be successful. I am grateful you are reading these pages. My hope is that you see the true heart of God differently and finally unlock your greatest gift, the power of choice. What's at stake for not being in alignment? A life that is unfulfilling, desperate, and causes households to fall apart because there is no leadership. Our world needs an army of men to start leading themselves, their families, and their communities better!

PART ONE

SACRIFICE

CHAPTER ONE

SACRIFICE IN THE WORLD TODAY

On a blistering hot Saturday morning, I awoke to the sound of water from an artesian well hitting the pond, birds chirping, and the rumbling of a diesel tractor engine. My heart sank knowing what that last sound, the diesel engine, really meant. On this particular Saturday, I was so excited to try out some new fishing lures, and test my craftiness in catching some large-mouth bass with my big brother Troy. But that tractor noise meant something very different needed to happen that day. I headed upstairs, pulled the cereal out of the pantry—frosted cheerios to be exact, and selected a large Tupperware bowl. The kind you definitely don't use for cereal. But who has time to pour multiple bowls of cereal when you know there is a better way? Halfway through my monstrous bowl of cereal, I heard the front door open and footsteps rushing up the stairs. To my surprise, it was Troy.

"Did you save any for the rest of us?" Troy blurted out.

"Of course, there is still half a box in the pantry!" I replied with a smirk.

"Troy, are you ready to go fishing?"

He looked at me with that face—you know, the one where your plans are about to be interrupted by an adult. "I don't think we can fish today because your dad's bailing hay, and we need to get out there before he has our hides." With a deep sigh, I knew he was right, but in my heart I wanted so badly to go fishing. Troy knew it too, because he was my teacher and fishing buddy.

Within a matter of minutes, the front door opened, and we heard what sounded like an angry grizzly bear's roar. "Would you two stop screwing around up there. We have hay to bail, so bring the tractor and wagon in about 20 minutes." There was no need to respond that I wanted to go fishing, because you don't argue with dad when he is upset and ready to work. So, Troy and I hooked up the tractor and wagon, and headed to the field where my dad was bailing hay, switched wagons, and headed home.

Now, learning how to cheat the system through sacrifice to have the best of both worlds, Troy said to me, "Go fishing and I will unload this wagon. When you hear me honk the horn, haul your butt up here fast, so we can go get another load. We will switch every other wagon, so we both can go fishing." I was so excited! This was genius! Hours went by, back and forth, unloading hay, and then everything fell apart. As I was casting across the pond, I heard a faint tractor noise, this one being different from the tractor Troy and I were using. Nevertheless, as a kid intent on becoming a master of catching fish, I disregarded it. Turning my focus back to the glass-like surface in front of me, I saw a large ripple! I hooked one, and it was big! I was determined to land this monster and prove my mastery. I was in another world fighting this monster made of legend and pictures, not noticing my father had come home, and was standing next to the house. Then boom, I heard a voice like thunder that shocked me out of my focus.

My heart sank and I knew I was in for it. My dad looked at me and uttered words I would take to heart, "We don't have time to be screwing around fishing when there is work to be done, so I better not catch you fishing again!" As my body trembled, not wanting him to be mad at me, I learned a valuable lesson: Work hard at any and all cost, and maybe, just maybe, you will have time to do what you want later. Make sacrifices now—give up fishing—to maybe have the hope of doing it later.

WEEDS AMONG GOOD SEEDS

The story of that day, while teaching me an unbelievably valuable lesson that has brought me much success in life, also shows a weed of deception planted among the good seed of hard work and sacrifice.

- Have you ever reflected on your life and asked yourself why the men you respected sacrificed things for you or their families?
- Where was their heart when they told you to make sacrifices?
- Was the way they lived their lives an example of the way God wants us to make sacrifices, or what the world says needs to be sacrificed?

As I began to ask myself these questions, I realized most of the things this world said would bring happiness and joy, were actually weeds. My father is my best friend, and the greatest man I know. Over years of reflecting on his life and mine, I realized he always made sacrifices because of responsibility to external circumstances. Learning my father's heart through the years showed me that he always wanted to travel, wanted to spend more time with us growing up, and wanted to give us more than he had. Yet watching him become more calloused as he gave up on the hopes and dreams God put in his heart, made me realize not all sacrifices are created equal.

You may say that is what every parent does for their children. As a new dad writing this book, I agree only partially with you. I believe the greatest deception for men in our world today is that we must sacrifice time away from our families, working jobs we are not passionate about, just to provide a certain lifestyle. A lifestyle that's only important because of what we didn't have, or what we thought we needed to keep up with worldly expectations or a false image. My father did what he was trained to do by the example that went before him. Men, we cannot blame those who came before us for the sacrifices they made!

> **We must seek to understand where their hearts were, and why the choices were made. Only then can we see their driving force and the ripple effects those choices have from generation to generation.**

What if you could ask the men who raised you where their hearts were when they walked away from your family, and why they sacrificed true manhood out of fear and selfishness? They may have been physically present, but emotionally they were not. The world has a way of saying, "Be a man, give up your family and time with them because you need to pay bills and put food on the table! That is how you can show them you care and love them!" This was another weed of false sacrifice planted among good seeds in my life. I watched men in my life sacrifice time and energy to support their families, from the world's perspective, yet when you looked in their eyes, they were lost and alone. Who they were called to be, and who they had to be, were growing worlds apart.

When I was about 25, I had a great friend who was married and had kids. We were in a business together, and we spent many days talking about how we would make millions one day to provide for our families. We were taught that, in order to have our dreams, our families must learn to have delayed gratification or sacrifice for future gain. We started to give up time with them, making sure they were submissive to the budget set forth to live minimally as we spent money traveling.

This all came to a head about a year later when they got divorced. It was a weird feeling watching a man start to lose his soul in pursuit of this world while thinking, if he makes just one more sacrifice for his family, they will have all their dreams. I tell you this story because this type of sacrifice is a weed—you neglect your responsibility to be present. Neglecting the emotions and hearts of your spouse, kids, and even yourself, for the hopes of filling an empty hole inside you. It is a sneaky and cunning way Satan hardens our hearts and misdirects us to continue to be void of true communion with God, and the relationships He has given us. Seeing this happen made me make an adjustment. I left my massive hopes and dreams behind, to stay present and be grateful. While this is another weed sown among the seed of gratitude, over time, we all do this. We chose to give up on the dreams God gave us to be present and grateful.

> **Life has a way of throwing us more than we can handle, and we think we can do it alone, yet years later, through pain and through worldly success, we realize we have buried our souls and the drive to live that God put deep inside us.**

Jesus told them another parable: "The kingdom of heaven is like a man who sowed good seed in his field. But while everyone was sleeping, his enemy came and sowed weeds among the wheat, and went away. When the wheat sprouted and formed heads, then the weeds also appeared. The owner's servants came to him and said, "Sir, didn't you sow a good seed in your field? Where then did the weeds come from?"

"An enemy did this," he replied.

The servants asked him, "Do you want us to go and pull them up?"

"No," he answered, "because while you are pulling the weeds, you may uproot the wheat with them. Let both grow together until the harvest. At that time, I will tell the harvesters: First, collect the weeds and tie them in bundles to be burned; then gather the wheat and bring it into my barn."[1]

Like many of you, I have read this passage a hundred times and didn't really understand it until I gave God my whole heart. He showed me, and I hope you can see it now too, that throughout our lives, Satan has a way of sowing weeds among the good seed. God has put good works inside of you, allows weeds to grow along with blessings He wants you to receive, and even will allow the weeds to remain until He wants to show you. Now, stop and see that the owner and his workers fell asleep! This was an overnight planting of destruction when they were mostly unaware. I imagine they slept well for many days as they prayed for rain and tended to other tasks. But it says when the wheat sprouted, the weeds did also. As men, many times in our lives, we sacrifice something like time away from our families to work for money to provide for our families, then come home and want to relax, or maybe we work overtime because the money is needed. Yet what we do not see is that there is a weed growing alongside the sacrifice of time, the weed of detachment. Detachment from our family's emotional needs and from trusting in our Father to provide for our every provision.[2]

It was at this point I would see my biggest mistake. I would see the weed of detachment and make excuses to my wife to justify why her needs were second to money and providing. You can see how, while there was a blessing of wheat (money), I tried to pull up the weed of detachment and ruined both by causing more damage to my family's heart, and also hardening mine in the process. This is what happens when we try to remove something before it's time; there are always consequences. I believe that is why in this parable Jesus is teaching us to become aware of the sacrifices we make, or those made for us over time.

There is a season coming where we will be able to separate what the world has sown in our hearts, and the blessing God wants to give us. A season when we need to wake up, separate the weeds from the good seed, and take responsibility for the choices we have made, even if those choices are ripple effects from other men in our lives.

CONSUMPTION OVERLOAD

The reason I am starting this book with sacrifice is to help shed some light on issues lying dormant in our hearts, and how we are continually misled. Sometimes we think about them and other times, they are subconscious habits. You may be asking, isn't sacrifice a good thing? We are told to give up today for the hopes of a better tomorrow, and as we consume, it never gets better.

This is misleading to many of us because, as we consume and give up our lives for others, without the right heart, we fall further away from who God made us to be. As men of God, we are called to steward our lives well, and to put others before ourselves. I say misleading because sacrifice in today's world is generally something tangible, yet we always forget the other side of the coin: who we are becoming!

I want to give you the definition of sacrifice, so we can be on the same page as we move along this journey to really understand the power behind what we give up. We all know what sacrifice means, or at least we think we do, until we gain another perspective, which then leads us to view the definition differently.

Merriam-Webster's definition of sacrifice—to suffer loss of, give up, renounce, injure or destroy for an ideal, belief, or end.

Take a moment, close your eyes, and let that definition sink into your heart. If you are anything like I am, this was the only definition I was taught throughout my life. The media we consume today through television, social media, magazines, and even fellow friends show us how to live in alignment with this definition. The average American spends a little over 2 hours a day watching TV,[3] which is also known as a program. We don't give this much thought as we laugh or are amused by reality TV. Yet we must understand that, since it is a program, there is an agenda. As we consume shows on how to remodel our homes, reality TV shows about how to quit our day jobs and chase entrepreneurship, and even shows on how dysfunctional families can be, we are subliminally programmed to this definition. As you have read in the last paragraph, I went from telling you these messages are programs to teach you to behave or think a certain way, and then changed the word program to show.

You may be asking yourself, "Why is that a big deal?"

It took me many years to see, as I consumed tv and movies, I was being programmed to think a certain way. You may have started off by saying, "Wow, we are being programmed!" But not stopping and giving a second thought that the word program was changed to show, we start to think of our favorite episode of 30 for 30, or our favorite Marvel Movie. What did this do? Because we "choose" to be inundated so quickly and consume information at a rapid pace, we become numb to how, through these subliminal changes, the world is changing, the men God created us to be.

In the movie The Bourne Identity, there is a special military project called Operation Treadstone. This program was meant to take individuals and give them extremely specific skill sets, to become weapons for the government for influence, control, and power. The movie opens with Jason Bourne, who had two gunshot wounds in his back, being rescued by a fishing vessel in the Mediterranean Sea. Jason, after gaining consciousness, has no memory of who he is, yet retained all of his combat skills and fluency in several languages. The captain asks Jason, "What is your name?"

Jason replies, "I don't know!"

Jason faints and is carried off to bed. Over the next several minutes, they show him reading maps, speaking in multiple languages, and helping work on the fishing vessel. Boom, it hit me! That was me! No, I did not get shot in the back twice, but I forgot who I was because of the programming given to me. I couldn't really remember the reasons I made sacrifices and how I got where I was. How was I able to continue being a warm body producing success, and yet forget why I was created? Who was I becoming? Why was I feeling empty inside? Was it because I was not living like the man God was asking me to be? This led me down a rabbit hole of questions. Much like Jason does throughout the movie, I started asking for God to show me who I was supposed to be, and how my choices got me where I was. What did I find?

God was standing there with me the whole time, but I couldn't see him due to consumption overload.

In a quiet moment, He spoke to me, saying, "Dustan, I created you to be powerful and with the right of free will and choice. You have chosen to make sacrifices without checking in with me, Bud! Your heart needs to be realigned, so please start from the beginning."

At that moment, I was so humbled, while being overcome with anger, because I genuinely thought what I was doing was the right way. So, listening to God's prompt, I started in Genesis; and that is when God doubled down, showing me the power and weight of my ability to choose! If you allow, I want to share with you the verse that started to pound on my heart. As I took my time reading from the beginning, I saw all the magnificent things God chose to create. He chose to create light that separated day and night. He chose to create a vault to separate water from the sky, and then chose to create land to separate the sea. As I read, I saw how powerful God's choices really are, because they show up in my life and the world I live in today. Then God made living creatures according to their kinds and livestock according to their kinds, and creatures that move along the ground according to their kinds. Then God said, "Let us make mankind in our image, in our likeness, so that they may rule over the fish in the sea and the birds in the sky, over the livestock and all the wild animals, and over all the creatures that move along the ground."[4] He **CHOSE** to create Man!

It's incredible that God chose to create us, and it moved me to pay attention to how powerful my choices really are. Likewise, God wants to be involved in my choices and, more importantly, with me in a relationship. It was while reading Genesis 2:19 that I fell to my knees and asked God to forgive me for sacrificing the wrong things in my life. "Now the Lord God had formed out of the ground all the wild animals and all the birds in the sky. He brought them to the man to see what he would name them; and whatever the man called each living creature, that was its name." Unbelievable!

> **God created everything, yet gave Adam the ability to name each and every living thing, and God didn't once question him.**

This absolutely rocked me! My hope is it will resonate with you also, to see that God wants you to pay attention to your choices because He has given you tremendous power. Power to control what goes into your heart and mind, power to do whatever you like, and power to choose who you want to become. So please, learn to set aside some time by shutting off your programs and smartphones, and begin to listen to the still small voice that is trying to lead you away from the unclean sacrifices that leave you hollow and empty.

UNCLEAN SACRIFICES

The world continues to dampen our understanding of a powerful weapon in our arsenal, sacrifice! However, to see what unclean sacrifices we have in our lives, we must go to the source for answers. What does God say is a clean sacrifice?

I ask you to read this next section with an open mind. As there is a context in any teaching, the perspective here is to understand in today's world, the disconnect between who we currently are and who God is asking us to become. In fact, I had to humble myself to understand how far short I was falling from who God was asking me to be. In the book of Leviticus, God instructs Moses what an acceptable sacrifice must be in order to redeem us of our sin and become right with God. Let us join Moses at the table as God sits across from us and gives us a lesson regarding sacrifice.

"When a ruler hath sinned, and done somewhat through ignorance against any of the commandments of the Lord his God concerning things which should not be done, and is guilty; Or if his sin, wherein he hath sinned, come to his knowledge; he shall bring his offering, a kid of the goats, a male without blemish…" Leviticus 4:22

Upfront! Personal! Challenging! The words used in the King James Version truly bring some weight to how God wants us to see our faults and humble us. It starts with "Ruler," and I love that because we are all rulers of our lives according to the life, death, and resurrection of Jesus. Believe in who God is saying you are. I would like to point out a few words describing what I sacrifice for God. I hope they get the wheels spinning for you, as they did for me.

- Ignorance
- Should not be done
- Is guilty
- Sin comes to his knowledge
- Male without blemish

Please stop for a moment and let those words and their weight seep into your heart! How many times do we make decisions, out of ignorance, regarding the direction of our daily lives? I have had way too many to list, as many of us men do—because of our ego.

> **You truly know what should not be done, yet refuse to listen to God speaking to you. He will show you after you have made the choice, though, where you have fallen short, and it may hurt a little.**

While the listed words and phrases start to shed light on areas where we have fallen short, I ask you to humble yourself and ask an honest question.

Why do I continue to make sacrifices that are not a "male without blemish?"

I asked myself this question for some time, and God showed me, time and time again, I had not brought my best to him. Searching for context on the "male without blemish," I learned God had asked for the best of every type of animal, not the worst or mediocre. He wanted to make sure if we did something wrong, we had to pay dearly for it. This may translate today through our relationships with our spouses. I am going to get brutally honest here, hoping my vulnerability will shed light on an area where you are sacrificing out of necessity instead of a place of honesty and your best.

I was married at 21, thinking I had the world by the horns! Thinking I knew what it took to be a husband and leader of my house, I asked my best friend at the time to marry me. Everything was great for us until my wife was in a car accident that would change me forever. I received a phone call that made my adrenaline spike, my heart race, and my knees buckle all at the same time. This is what I heard:

"Dustan, I was in an accident!"

My heart sank. At that moment, the only thought I had was, "Is she ok?" I headed to her immediately. When I arrived on the scene, it looked like barely more than a fender bender. But as I got out of the car and heard the story, I learned she was hit at a dead standstill by a person having a diabetic attack, going 60mph! The grace of God had protected her at that moment, and my mind was blown. However, this was a moment where my heart began to harden toward God, and a weed was planted.

Despite many hospital visits and chiropractic adjustments over the next couple of years, she was not getting better. I was working many odd jobs to pay the bills that never stopped coming. I sacrificed time I should have been spending with my hurting wife by feeling it was more important to keep a roof over our heads and food on the table, than tending to the needs of a physically wounded daughter of God. My heart grew angry with God while my dreams were disappearing at a rapid rate. I felt I was not only losing who He called me to be on that mountain in Colorado, but also believing these things were happening because he either wanted me to suffer, or He just didn't care.

Over the next nine years of ups and downs, the weed of sacrificing my time to make money, seeking relationships that were unhealthy, and neglecting my responsibilities as a Godly man, my marriage ended in divorce. Looking back, there were moments of good where God protected me, and there were many moments where I brought to Him only what I thought was necessary for His approval. This came in the form of going to church on Sunday yet never spending time with Him any other day, making sales in my job that went against my integrity to gain popularity or money, in hopes it would change the issues in my relationship, or sacrificing to my marriage and friends, a false image of who I really was. Now you may be asking, "Why are these things 'unclean sacrifices?'"

I hadn't ever brought my true heart to any area of my life, or to God for that matter. I was giving up only what was necessary to make it to the next day. This was not what God meant in speaking with Moses about bringing an "unblemished male."

> **It was more like, "I will give you, God, what I can deal without, halfheartedly and out of ignorance to what you're trying to do in my heart and life."**

Continuing to sacrifice what was not my best, sacrificing what did not advance His Kingdom, sacrificing my integrity to get ahead, honestly broke me! I started to see how what I was bringing to God was unclean—like slapping Him in the face for all He had done in my life.

Brothers, as you look back at your lives and see the unclean sacrifices, as you see the weeds planted among the good seeds in your life, and you control what you consume into your heart, may this prayer give you strength! May it help you assess your choices and let God begin to send you on the journey to recover proper alignment with His will for you.

Father God, thank You for all You are! Thank You for showing us, as men, the pitfalls and unclean sacrifices of our lives, that cause us to fall short of what you ask. Thank You, Father God, for sending Your only son, Jesus, to be that perfect unblemished man that bridged that gap of your love and mercy. May You show my heart and soul which areas I need to give to You through humility and prayer. As I walk this journey of awareness, Father, may Your presence overcome me; and may I have the eyes to see and the ears to hear Your will over the world's shouting. Father, thank You for the power of choice YOU gave Adam and Your son, Jesus, and may I use that same power to move Your kingdom forward and the kingdom You have given me stewardship over to its greatest state. Father, I love you and am on my knees knowing that only through You will my heart be whole, and the ship I am sailing be righted. Thank You for Your grace, love, and protection over my life and those I love, in Jesus' name. Amen.

BATTLE PLAN CHAPTER 1

1. What have you sacrificed in your life that was for the wrong reason?
2. Looking back at your past, can you see lessons of sacrifice that the world said were good, yet have caused pain and left you empty? List them, then write down a better sacrifice next to the first, that aligns more with who you want to become. (i.e., sacrificed time away from family for work—better sacrifice was making your family a priority and managing your time and efficiency better while at work.)
3. There are weeds that are growing along with the good seeds you have planted in your life. Take a look at the good seed and see what bad seed is there, address it, and be ready to burn it when the time comes. (i.e., good seed = wanting more by working hard, weed = selfishness – how can you continue to work hard yet checking your motives?)
4. God created you for great things, yet always remember you get the choice of what you put in your heart. Cut down on what you consume through the media and replace it with 10-20 minutes of reading or dreaming.

CHAPTER TWO

WHY SUCCESS, YET NEVER FULFILLMENT?

"Yet the Brilliance of God is that the false self becomes less and less capable of producing the life we seek." Morgan Snyder

It was November 2015, my divorce was final, and I had put in a transfer to another division in Florida with the company I worked for. As I took the long drive, I felt relieved I could run away from my past, God, and who I used to be. Back in full swing were dreams and ambitions to prove I could make it big in a different part of the country, without God, and in a relationship I should not have been in. They say, "Hindsight is 20/20," and "You live and learn." But at what cost? Looking back on those choices it cost me the man God was trying to save! It cost me time from my family, almost cost me my job because of my ego, and cost me precious time healing from the wounds I was not willing to address.

Before I left Wisconsin, I was a successful salesman making great money. My walk with God, as I have mentioned previously, was give and take—by that I mean, "God, please give me... and I'll take what I want." Grooming myself through the skills and self-development books of others, I became numb to others, and who they were created to be. I manipulated situations to get what I wanted. "That's very selfish and evil," you may be thinking. While that is true, I did what I felt I needed to do to survive. Listening to the world's view of sacrifice turned me into a machine with no heart, like the Tinman in the *Wizard of Oz*. If that movie reference is too old for some, let me say it turned me into Tony Stark in *Iron Man*, before he was captured in the middle east and saw what his legacy had become.

Now that I think of it, Tony is definitely a better example. While I haven't had fancy cars or a penthouse with cool gadgets, in my heart, I felt I was invincible, untouchable, and could take whatever I wanted in this life. One of the greatest scenes in that movie was when Tony, with a helper named Yinsen, was building a device in the cave. Tony realized he needed to survive, and it was now or never. Being aware of the reality of his situation: to keep his heart beating, but also to escape capture, he turned himself into something no one had ever seen. He jumped into a huge suit of armor, which was powered by a battery and kept shrapnel out of his heart, blasts down the doors, and starts to kick some serious bad-guy butt!

If you are a movie fan or even a fan of good guys kicking butt, this scene stirs your heart to become something different, and take back what was taken from you—your freedom. Your heart pumps, your brain is saying you were built for this, so you show them who's boss. For a moment, you feel as if you are walking in that giant suit of armor. That is how I felt moving to Florida and becoming who I needed to be in the world's eyes to succeed and feel worth. Now I am sure you can relate. It may not be this movie, but there is a point in your favorite movie where you become the character and feel what he feels! Become who he becomes in that moment of struggle and triumph and look toward your enemy, saying, "You have no idea the can I am about to open on you!"

Let us come back to reality a little and understand why I bring up this story in the first place. You are picturing power and success, yet forgetting what I mentioned regarding my motivation; I moved to run away from God and who He was asking me to be. God never forces us to follow Him. He will always give us the CHOICE. Even if that means letting us become part of this world, so He could teach us something far greater once we have fallen to our knees. This was best illustrated when Tony came back from being rescued and sat on the ground in front of the podium at his press conference. That was when he finally understood that all the money, power, and fame he and his father built in the manufacturing of weapons was now worthless to him. Tony proceeded to shut down the manufacturing division of weapons effective immediately to pursue a better way. Now for those who have watched this amazing movie, you know he builds the Iron Man suit and takes on a whole new persona, with a different purpose.[1]

When I look back on this movie, God showed me what the world is truly capable of. It makes you believe you have to be a specific kind of success, which it programs you for very early in life; and then, when it matters most, it leaves you in a cave to find a way to survive. My heart truly breaks daily for each and every man who chases value and worth through success in this life.

> **There are so many of us who continue to strive to fill a hole in our hearts that was never meant for us to fill on our own.**

Every day we chase this world and become more successful; we lose pieces of the true nature of a man that God intended when He breathed life into our bodies.

In the book *Becoming A King*, author Morgan Snyder touches on this in reference to the false self or the worldly man in us. He describes it this way:

"The false self is a careful construct crafted largely to avoid shame and fear and make life work apart from God. As we are being formed, external problems often help reveal places within us that need to be tended to. The brilliance of God's design for masculine initiation is that the more we truly want life as it was meant to be, the less efficient the false self becomes in producing what feels like life."[2]

Honestly, think about the quote above! As you continue to allow the false self or worldly self to control how you will be defined, the further away from your purpose you go. This showed me that, the more I strive for the things of this world, the more I ignore the problems I should have tended to in my soul. The world has a nasty way of separating us from God, yet as Morgan said, the brilliance of God is to show us a better way. He does that by giving us examples in David, Elijah, Paul, and Jesus, and most importantly, helping us be fulfilled when we seek Him with the right heart.

SAUL BEFORE HE WAS PAUL

One of the greatest examples we have of someone striving to be of this world and being successful in it comes from Saul of Tarsus. Saul was a lot like most of us men who seek to conquer in today's world. We want to be known, have status, be feared, and most of all, become whole through these worldly successes. Saul was born in modern-day Turkey to Jewish parents who had Roman citizenship, and he became a great student of Hebrew Scriptures and the Law. His life's work was to persecute those who did not follow the law, and he was good at it! So good that the historian Luke tells us in Acts 7:58 Stephen's accusers, one by one, placed their outer garments at the feet of Saul while stoning him outside the city walls. He was a modern-day boss and enforcer in regard to the Jewish law. Respected and feared, full of ego and pride, he lived amongst this world as many of us do today. I identified with who Saul was in his quest for greatness and finding various forms of success; do you? Are you aiming for this?

I firmly believe God shows us Saul, as an example of how strong our lineage and history really are in shaping our false sense of success. You could say, if he had continued to do what he was doing in persecuting the church, he might have had a great career in doing so. But would he have been fulfilled? Was Saul living in alignment with the proper sacrifices to live a Godly life? The answer to that would be no! He was making sacrifices to an outdated Law that no longer carried the same weight it once did. How does this relate to you and me? God wants you to see that chasing this world as Saul did, will hurt you more than help you. Sacrifices made from outdated information, the way our parents used to do things, or the way the media conditions us to think, will leave every man alone and empty. That is why I related so much with Saul because I had all these things, and my heart was unaware of the eternal choices I was making. Remember, I told you I ran from God; and in the same way, Saul was doing things based on what the world told him. I needed to sacrifice to get ahead to feel, in some way—whole!

Take courage here men and leaders! We have sacrificed our time in this world for the wrong outcomes, but that does not mean this is the end for us. There is more to the story for Saul, and there is for you too! Let us finish the story here. Understand, God loves you and is trying to interrupt your life to redeem the sacrifices you made for the wrong reasons. He shows us this in Acts 9:3-9, God changed Saul on the road to Damascus by interrupting his plans to persecute more Christians. A flash of light appeared and asked:

"Saul, Saul, why are you persecuting me?"

Saul replied, "Who are you, Lord?"

"I am Jesus, the Victorious, the one you are persecuting. Now, get up and go into the city, where you will be told what you are to do."

Thankfully, we are not made blind when God interrupts our lives! I do believe He is trying to get our attention, to awaken us, so we'll realize the sacrifices we continually make have consequences. He wants to bring us into alignment with His true purpose for our lives, and the lives of those around us.

PERFECT INTERRUPTIONS

We are halfway through the first section, and I cannot stress enough, the importance of bringing clarity to your life. That may be why the first chapter and a half are a little more on the aggressive side. The greatest thing I have learned is, if we do not have clarity, we do not know how to move forward to live a different life. I love each of you and care so much for where your eternity lies.

> **I do not want you spending your days making sacrifices that don't add to your treasures in heaven, not to mention leading those astray whom you are meant to care for.**

Over the next chapter and a half, we will venture down the road of good sacrifices, and help you see there are things God loves more than the sacrifices you can make. Buckle up and get ready for the download of good choices with the right sacrifices to move the needle forward in your life.

Jesus blinded Saul for a time, and then later, when his eyes were opened, something like scales fell off.[3] Saul then began preaching and growing in his faith and leading the very people he had previously persecuted into a stronger faith. In studying Saul's life, we see Saul was sent to Cyprus and then started using his Roman name, Paul. Let me be clear: nowhere did Jesus change Paul's name like he did Abraham's from Abram.[4] It was after this event in Cyprus Paul chose to go by his Roman name, enabling him to relate to the Gentiles with whom he was commissioned to share the Gospel. When you look at the life of Saul, you see God's perfect interruption of love to help send him on the path to his true purpose.

I really believe God perfectly interrupts our lives to show us when the way we are going is not good. He did this in a big way in my life, that really helped me realign with good sacrifices. While reflecting on the brokenness of my heart through my divorce, toxic relationships, and lack of success, God gave me my perfect interruption. One day as I was walking around the block to calm my thoughts and heart, I came to a church conducting a Wednesday night service. Being angry at God and mistaking my poor choices as losing favor from my Father in heaven, I was at odds within myself to walk back into a church again. Yet something inside me so calmly nudged me, almost as if he were saying, "Please just hear what I have to say." He knew I was in pain and suffering because I lived by my sacrifices to get ahead! This was the perfect opportunity to give me a word that would change the way I would walk out my faith.

As I sat there in pain and remorse in the far back of the church where no one could see me, these words were spoken:

"Therefore, I urge you, brothers and sisters, in view of God's mercy, to offer your bodies as living sacrifices, holy and pleasing to God—this is your spiritual act of worship." Romans 12:1

The pastor was teaching that we need to take our every-day lives, our words, our jobs, our relationships and place them before God as an offering, a good sacrifice. I broke down, tears falling from my face. God interrupted my path to show me a better way. Ripped open emotionally, I did not even stay for the whole service. I walked around for an hour, trying to make sense of what God was showing me.

Over the next several years, God opened my eyes, much like Paul's, to what really mattered to Him. To give every moment that I have breath in my lungs to the one who wasn't asking that I sacrifice my life for this world, but lay it at His feet daily so that he could bless my steps.

I ask you to pause and think about the questions below, knowing now that the only Sacrifice your Father in Heaven wants from you is to humble yourself and live for Him.

- Why do you say one thing and do another?
- Why do you sacrifice your time away from your family to earn more money?
- What have you been giving to others that you wish you had or did not?
- What is your greatest regret in things you have done?
- Why do you give your energy to everything around you, yet continue to run on empty?

I know where you are in the chaos and confusion of the world we live in. That is also why I believe now your eyes are open and you are ready to see clearly. There is hope! A hope that in honestly answering the questions above God will also perfectly interrupt you. He will give you comfort from the pain of sacrificing the best of you for a world that never cared. May he give you His perfect grace to start walking a new path.

NOW WHAT?

In the search for answers over those next couple of years, I saw what great sacrifices were made by those around me, and the good sacrifices I made in my life. There are four areas I focused on, so I could become that living sacrifice Paul described. Though they are not easy, and I sometimes still fail at them, God began to restore my heart and prepare me for my next journey. My prayer for you is they will seep into your heart to bring strength and momentum for what God has in store for you in your next season.

1. Our Words, or lack thereof

Proverbs 18:21 "Death and life are in the power of the tongue, and those who live it will eat its fruits."

In the process of becoming the living sacrifice God was pleased with, I knew the story I told myself and others needed to change. I started to live by the world's standards in how I got ahead in life, and we both know that comes from a twisted tongue. James Allen probably said this best in As a Man Thinketh: "As he thinks, so he is; as he continues to think, so he remains." This changed my heart. Realizing the power of my words to myself and others, was why I was empty and making sacrifices that brought more suffering than joy. As you start walking on this journey to making better choices, pay attention to the words you're speaking over yourself and others, because that "fruit" will always be eaten. As I began searching my words, I could see I was not praising God for all the good he did for me. I was not lifting others up through my words to give them life. Change the words you speak and where your praise goes, and watch how God changes your life!

2. Service and sharing

Hebrews 13:16 "And do not forget to do good and to share with others, for with such sacrifices, God is pleased."

It's ridiculously hard for anyone who is sacrificing to get ahead by the standards of this world, to share and do good things for others. This is my greatest gift and my greatest weakness. For so long, I thought that when I was serving others, they would appreciate me more and reciprocate in some way to make it a two-way street. Yet, that is not what the writer of Hebrews is telling us. When the position of your heart is truly to do good because it's the right thing to do, and to share what you have either by material or spiritual gifts, you are advancing the kingdom in a way no one can argue with. I noticed my heart became full of life, knowing there was only one person I was serving—Jesus. So in the busyness of life, do not forget to do something for someone else today, and feel how it will ignite a spark inside you for more!

3. Physical health

Hebrews 10:5 "Therefore, when Christ came into the world, he said: 'Sacrifice and offering you did not desire, but a body you prepared for me;'" I really resonated with the humility of Jesus saying, "a body you prepared for me." This made me examine things having effects on my body, and how I was destroying what God prepared this vessel to do. After reading that, I was led to 1 Corinthians 6:19-20 "Do you not know that your bodies are temples of the Holy Spirit, who is in you, whom you have received from God? You are not your own; you were bought at a price. Therefore, honor God with your bodies." WOW!!!! At this stage of my life, I was in a bad place. I was 310lbs and miserable. My energy and ability to feel good about myself were low, and the consequences of not taking care of the body God prepared for me were beyond evident. When was the last time you gave your body a service? Just like our vehicles need to be cared for and regularly serviced to go the distance, so do we. The only difference here is you can buy a new car, but you only get one body. When I got serious about getting my body back into a healthy place, my joy and energy began to skyrocket! Please remember, "You cannot share what you first do not experience." If you want to do good and share with others, then take care of yourself; and you will have the energy required to share the joy and health you experience firsthand.

4. Grace with yourself

As someone who honestly has the hardest time with forgiveness, especially with myself, this was the drop of water that made the rock of my heart crack. God knew I would always be my biggest critic, and until I could fully understand I was always going to fall short of his perfect love for me, I was going to struggle. There are going to be days where you will fail so badly you will not want to walk out of the house for a week! You will be laughed at, mocked, and you will not live up to your own expectations of yourself. That is ok! I am here to tell you—and you can ask my wife—I always feel that I could have said something different in a conversation, stepped up and served someone with more of my time, or stayed up later trying to excavate my heart to find the man God created me to be. The problem with this type of reflection, while it is a great attribute to have in pushing yourself to become a better person, is it swallows all the little victories we have. More importantly, removes God's grace from the picture. The days I woke up remembering I needed His grace, were the days I started out winning.

> **Even more than winning, those days started in a place of peace that could only come from knowing I am not perfect, but daily loving the man who is: Jesus.**

Here are some scriptures that brought me peace amidst my own judgment and failures. My hope is you can stand on these truths to see

God's grace moving in your heart and the choices you make.

Philippians 3:13 "But this one thing I do, forgetting those things which are behind, and reaching forth unto those things which are before."

Psalm 103:10-12 "He does not treat us as our sins deserve or repay us according to our iniquities. For as high as the heavens are above the earth, so great is the love for those who fear him; as far as the east is from the west, so far has he removed our transgressions from us."

2 Corinthians 5:17-18 "So from now on we regard no one from a worldly point of view. Though we once regarded Christ in this way, we do so no longer. Therefore, if anyone is in Christ, the new creation has come: the old has gone, the new is here!"

Let God step into these words and please stand on them yourselves. The process of change and forgiving ourselves for our empty sacrifices and choices will be a daily battle, yet the hope above is showing us that, with a little patience and grace, we can be restored. Restored because of how much our Father in heaven truly loves us, and will finish the good works He started in us.

What are you going to do with the daily second chance you are given? How will you choose to love over sacrifice? What will it take for you to give your best to a Father who has seen you at your worst?

The greatest part in this journey of understanding alignment with God's purpose, was when God showed me the word obedience. I spent time in the first two chapters to help you see the issues of sacrificing for the world. These kinds of unclean sacrifices will never fulfill you. They will only reveal a selfish love that continues to break your heart, and walk you further and further away from your purpose. Hopefully, with this new-found awareness from the walls you have torn down in your world of sacrifice, this next chapter will propel you to discover a zest for life that can only come when we submit to something greater than ourselves.

Father, thank You for showing us where our hearts fall short, and why we make sacrifices that bring worldly fulfillment for a time, yet leave us empty and hurting. Thank You for Your son Jesus, who has bought and paid for my stupidity with the most perfect sacrifice of all, dying so I may know you personally. Father, thank You for helping me see Your grace and love as I start to live more focused for you and continue to feel Your presence in my life daily. Lord, I give my past to You; may you restore my present, and may I walk with You into the future You have planned for me. Thank You for giving me the chance to make choices that will put me into better alignment with You, and bring your level of joy into every corner of my heart.

In this moment of humility and restoration, please search for the song "Graves into Gardens" by Elevation Worship. Give praise to God through these amazing words, as He has already begun the process of turning your graves into gardens that bear fruit you never knew you could bear!

BATTLE PLAN CHAPTER 2

1. What are some things you're striving for that are not fulfilling your soul, and leading you closer to your purpose?
2. Has God been trying to get your attention through a "perfect interruption?" Look back at your life and see if He has already interrupted you, but you missed it because you were focused on this world. Write down those interruptions, and see how God has been trying to get your attention this whole time.
3. Just like Saul becoming Paul, you too, are putting off the old. Write down three old things you were either chasing or becoming. Now write down who the new person, the true child of God, is becoming! Hold this list with you, and know you're not defined by who you were or what you did in the past. God does not keep a record of your wrongs! Neither should you!
4. What is holding you back from giving yourself as a living sacrifice for God? Take stock of what is holding you back, write it down, crumble it up, and make the choice to give Him all you have. Don't let these fears, past choices, or wrong sacrifices deter you from the best choice you could ever make! On the other side is true freedom!

PART TWO

OBEDIENCE

CHAPTER THREE

HALF-HEARTED DECISIONS

Today's world has created a misrepresentation of one of the most powerful words ever given to mankind. I am going to do my best to illustrate what I mean throughout this chapter, within the story of Saul's life. It's a story we have all heard, but I am hopeful you will see it a little differently now. As I mentioned in the earlier chapter, the power of this one word changed how I chose to live my life every single day. To set the tone for the next two chapters, take a look at the definition of "obedience" first. Allow this to resonate in your soul, let the walls fall in regard to what you think it really means, and let God help draw you closer to him.

Obedience:
- The state or quality of being obedient
- The act or practice of obeying; dutiful or submissive compliance

MISDIRECTION

As I write this book, the year is 2020—one most of us wish to erase from our memories forever. We were hit with the Covid-19 pandemic at the end of March, which is when we started to see the true misunderstanding of the word obedience. As politicians began to jockey for position in the upcoming election, decisions carried more weight than they ever have in my lifetime. First, the country shut down completely to stop the spread of what some believe to be a man-made virus. Since I have been alive, I cannot remember a time when the United States shut down! Through fear tactics such as bullying, misinformation, and attacking people's livelihoods, the human soul has been split in two.

As we watched racial discrimination play out all over every news outlet, our trust in humanity grew faint. Riots ensued and businesses were burned to the ground, glass shattered all over the street, and neighborhoods turned into pure chaos, for what? These violent distractions directed our attention away from the law and order that once encompassed our country, but more importantly, away from the ultimate authority of our Heavenly Father. This was not the only time in history that our enemy has tried to misdirect us or divide our hearts, in relation to our alignment with our Heavenly Father. I want to show you a piece of scripture that catapulted me forward in writing this book. If you have made it this far, I commend you on being patient with me, and honoring your Father in heaven to pursue understanding. This is where we start to grasp what happens when we are misled by the world around us and even by our fleshly nature.

There was a handsome man that came from the tribe of Benjamin. He was appointed by God to be King of Israel because of the people's lack of faith and obedience. The people wanted a king in the flesh, so that is exactly what God gave them. Samuel, a prophet of God, gave Saul a message concerning Israel, saying, "Has not the Lord anointed you ruler over his inheritance?"[1] As we understand Saul's journey, God would use Saul to save Israel from their enemies, and this would be a sign that He anointed Saul as ruler over the people. When I read this, I saw how amazing it would be to have God show you his heart and give you his promise for the direction of your life. Through the rest of the story, I realized that he was actually trying to do that for me too, if I would just listen.

Saul led Israel to victory over the course of many battles. As he became more powerful and wealthy, his heart became half-in with God's original purpose for his life—to rule over God's people. At the same time, the people of Israel were also upset and weary of now having someone to submit to other than God, even though that is what they asked for. Samuel proceeds to make it very clear to both the people and the new King Saul, that "If you fear the Lord and serve and obey him and do not rebel against his commands, and if both you and the King who reigns over you follow the Lord your God—Good! But if you do not obey the Lord, and if you rebel against his commands, his hand will be against you, as it was against your ancestors."[2]

What a stern warning regarding disobedience to both authorities in this passage. It speaks to the nature of each of us, that we want the blessings of God yet only want to do it when we want. Remember the old saying, "what goes around, comes around?" The people, much like us men today, didn't want an actual king or an authority to submit to. What they wanted was someone to fight their battles for them, so they could reap the rewards of an easy life. How many times do we turn a blind eye to the selfish nature in our hearts because we are unwilling to fight, unwilling to submit to an authority that has never lost a battle?

REBELLION

As we will soon learn, we are not alone in this fight against our selfish nature to rebel against authority. Saul went into battle as the prophet had told him, yet when he saw that his men were scattering, he became afraid that the Philistines would overcome him. He took the burnt offerings and sacrificed them to God.[3] Samuel showed up just after Saul had done this and rebuked him by saying, "You have done a foolish thing. You have not kept the command the Lord, your God gave you; if you had, he would have established your kingdom over Israel for all time. But now your kingdom will not endure; the Lord has sought out a man after his own heart and appointed him ruler of his people, because you have not kept the Lord's command."[4]

Ouch!! I pray that none of us ever gets a lesson in humility and faith like this:

> **To have someone that is a mentor say that our kingdom has been removed from us and given to another. Saul's lack of obedience to authority is something we can relate to. We tend to go through our lives trying to make decisions with half of our heart.**

We do not rely on the King of Kings to show up on heaven's time. This decision from Saul removed him from his kingdom. For me, my kingdom fell because I didn't submit my whole heart to God. I was divorced, no kids, working a job that was unfulfilling, and 1100 miles from my family. When my eyes were fully opened to my disobedience, and half-hearted approach to living a life for Christ, I could see Saul's heart in me. God had blessed my life. He gave me a kingdom to rule, but I was not the man he asked me to be to lead it. We are not alone in this separation from the greatest power and ruler on earth or in heaven.

There are many men over the course of history who have fallen away in disobedience, and each carried consequences. Adam, the first man, disobeyed God and ate from the Tree of Knowledge of Good and Evil—man fell from grace.[5] Saul disobeyed God's commands by lacking faith in battle, and leaving a king alive whom God said to remove from this life—he was removed from his kingdom, and his legacy did not endure. David disobeyed God by ordering the death of Uriah—it's forever attached as a blemish to his greatness and his first child with Bathsheba died as punishment.[6] Adonijah disobeyed his father David, and appointed himself as a false king—his brother Solomon replaced him, and Adonijah and his followers were killed.[7] Peter denied Jesus three times—which led to him running away and hiding in disgrace.[8] Each of these men had the opportunity to realign with authority. As we know, some did, but some grew further from God.

Just like the men of history, our choice to rebel leads to consequences that hurt our intimate relationship with our Father, and with those in our kingdom who are entrusted to us. The consequences of our half-hearted obedience , sometimes come to fruition much later. Our habits of walking out of the covering of God's grace lead to divorce, losing our jobs, kids growing up without fathers, the loss of integrity, and even life in some cases.

THE ULTIMATE CONSEQUENCE

While Saul was still the acting King, God removed Saul's reign and gave it to a man after God's own heart.[9] Now, while this may not seem like much, let's follow Saul's final fall, and examine where God had enough of his selfish decisions. We will see his consequences come to a head with God's true purpose for his life, and all of ours. The weight of the words to follow are glanced over by most, but since you're still here traveling down this road of understanding, may they be amplified in your soul. May you see your life, and your Heavenly Father, from a new perspective.

We pick up this story in 1 Samuel 15, where God gave direct orders to Saul, to banish the Amalekites from existence. He was commanded by Samuel to obey the command of the Lord and remove the group of people for all the pain and suffering they caused Israel when they left Egypt. Saul knew that when God gave a command, he was to obey, so he led his army to eliminate them. Instead of coming back, he went to Carmel, where he built a monument in his own honor![10] As Samuel met Saul, Saul proceeded to boast that he had done as the Lord instructed. Only one problem, Samuel heard the bleating of sheep and knew that Saul was lying. This mistake of not eliminating the Amalekites and everything they had, turned out to have consequences that would change all of our lives forever. Saul tried to justify his actions, like most of us do when we are caught not being men of integrity or obedience. He told Samuel that the men took only the best to sacrifice to God as burnt offerings. I imagine Saul standing there proud and feeling like he can make it out of this. Then he says he even brought King Agag. Bad move! How many of us try to justify our decisions even though we know we are wrong? On the road of consequences, when do you insert foot to mouth? Saul didn't and most of the time we do not either, until it's too late.

The next words spoken by Samuel, given to him by God, are what truly changed the way I understood the power of my choices. Please don't miss this. Meditate on these words, and be still enough to hear what God is trying to tell you!

"Does the Lord delight in burnt offerings? To obey is better than sacrifice, and to heed is better than the fat of rams." 1 Samuel 15:22

What did God tell you? What is stirring in your soul?

When the veil was torn from these words I crumbled. It rocked me to realize that God makes each of us kings in the kingdom he provides, and all He is asking is that we obey Him. I saw my life flash before me, highlighting all the ways I, like Saul, chose to make sacrifices that I thought God would want from me, yet I truly missed the mark. I continually fell away from His grace because I missed something so simple, yet so profound. If this is also you, your heart and soul can now see that you're out of alignment. Stay in that space. Stay in the emotions that you have and let them break down walls. Let them show you why you have been half-hearted, why you choose not to submit to the author and perfecter of your faith.

There is hope in this moment of seeing your life the way God sees it. Awareness and humility allow God to help you in this vulnerability, and lead you on the path of restoration. Before we start to walk down that road, I need to bring one more passage to light to drive home the results of our actions. May you never hear these words, may you take your walk seriously, may you start to walk in alignment before it's too late.

Saul pleaded with Samuel to come back with him and worship God for forgiveness, tore Samuel's cloak, and then these words were spoken,[11] "The Lord has torn the kingdom of Israel from you today and has given it to one of your neighbors—to one better than you." 1 Samuel 15:28

As I read these words over and over, I started to see that my actions would lead me to ex-communication from the kingdom. In my humility and brokenness, I pleaded with God not to give my purpose, my kingdom, to someone that was better than I was! If you're a man and these words above do not cut into the deepest part of your being, your wood is wet! As men, we are called to be strong, love deeply, and protect those in our care. The question is, are you? Do you want your life to become less than what it should be? Are you willing, because of ego and pride, to give your kingdom to someone better than you?

I know these are bold questions, and please know, I struggled to answer them honestly. The last thing any of us men want to hear is that our spouse is leaving because she found someone better, our kids like hanging out with their friend's parents because they are better, or maybe you apply for a promotion and learn it was given to someone better! All the while, knowing you are the best, there will never be someone better than you! If that is what you think then we are getting somewhere! Now let us start to use the energy that is brewing in your spirit to get back into line with what God tells us matters most—obediently listening to Him.

A-TEN-TION!!

The military is one of the best representations of obedience. As the drill sergeant barks out, "attention!" everyone snaps into line, face forward, in a posture of respect. Here are some ways that I believe can help each of us start to process and correct our current course, so that our purpose is not given up to someone better than we are in God's eyes.

FORGIVENESS

The only way up from here is forgiveness. We need to come back to our Father and ask him to restore us, and seat us once again on the throne. He will grant you that forgiveness because he loves you, and genuinely wants to have a relationship with you. You are his child, and not only has he already forgiven you, but he has also forgotten it happened. For us, forgetting it happened, and finding a way to forgive ourselves, is the tougher issue. We tend to beat ourselves up over what has been done, even though we cannot change the past. We are called to press on to what is ahead, to run our race. But the only way to do that is to look in the mirror and say out loud, "I forgive you of your past choices! I forgive you for being disobedient!"

> **God has restored you and has a hope and a future for you! This is not something that will be done once and everything is golden going forward. A daily commitment to forgive ourselves is crucial to finding freedom in God's grace.[12]**

The second part of forgiveness is the forgiveness of others. When I was honest with myself and asked God to show me those that I needed to forgive, he did. I started to see that the choices of the men in my life and their interactions with me, or lack thereof, was not the weight I was meant to carry.

Forgiving those who have hurt you or led you astray, brings freedom to your soul. When you make a choice to forgive, whether you tell them or not, you are released from spirits of anger, resentment, fear, anxiety, and hate. This allows you to draw a line in the sand, grab your Heavenly Father's hand, and let the weight of the past sink into the depths of history. It's good to always remind ourselves that we are not who we once were and will not be defined by what we have done. Start today. Take a moment right now, take a deep breath and forgive those you need to, so that God can bring your heart and soul back to balance.

Here are some words of encouragement to stand on regarding forgiveness:

"For if you forgive other people when they sin against you, your heavenly Father will also forgive you. But if you do not forgive others their sins, your Father will not forgive your sins." Matthew 6:14-15

"Get rid of all bitterness, rage, and anger, brawling and slander, along with every form of malice. Be kind and compassionate to one another, forgiving each other, just as in Christ God forgave you." Ephesians 4:31-32

"If we confess our sins, he is faithful and just and will forgive us our sins and purify us from all unrighteousness." 1 John 1:9

"Repent, then, and turn to God, so that your sins may be wiped out, that times of refreshing may come from the lord." Acts 3:19

HUMILITY

Humility was described to me as coming to the understanding of what you do not know. When we humbly come to God and realize that we don't know everything, that we no longer want to control outcomes, and honestly want to gain wisdom from the source—it is here where the heart is mended.

In this special place, we find the compassion to see the world from God's eyes. We see the eternal view to our short lives, and how much we need to rely on God to help guide our steps. When you are in this tender space, God will not leave you. As he showed me, He will lean into you and your life. Humility with God is like a young child and its parents. We watch as they ask questions, fall and get back up, and learn to make better decisions. This is where we need to return to in our relationship with our Father, and He will bless our obedience to his word by always giving us our daily bread.

As men, humility within ourselves is important, because all too often, it contends with pride. To become aware in the battle for your obedience, allows your Father to wage war against the unseen, and gives you the wisdom to walk in alignment with His will for you. What would happen if you took the promise literally, the promise that "If you ask, you shall receive?"[13] What would your life be like if you came humbly to every person you meet like a child, asking questions and eager to learn, with no agenda other than to gain wisdom? This changes our perspective on relationships as well as our walk with God, because it puts our heart in a posture to grow.

Stand on these scriptures to gain humility and strength.

"Humble yourselves before the Lord and he will lift you up in honor." James 4:10

"If my people, who are called by my name, will humble themselves and pray and seek my face and turn from their wicked ways, then I will hear from heaven, and I will forgive their sin and will heal their land." 2 Chronicles 7:14

"The greatest among you will be your servant. For those who exalt themselves will be humbled, and those who humble themselves will be exalted." Matthew 23:11-12

RESPONSIBILITY

Now that we see where we truly are in our life and our walk with God, one thing remains: one of the most powerful choices our Creator has given us is the ability to respond.

> **We must look back and be grateful for what we have gone through because it has shaped us to be who we are at this very moment.**

While some of our choices have not been the best, and others have brought great rewards, each of us has a duty to ourselves and those around us, to respond better to what is brought our way. This allows us to lead better in our relationships, our work, and in our personal walk with Christ. God will allow us to have more than we can handle in our lives, both struggle and success, to see how we respond to each event in relation to Him. When we become truly aware that our ability to respond can honor Him in a way that brings joy to his heart and abundance to our character, our faith is perfected in Him who so freely gives. Take courage in this because you and I will continue to fall short. At times, we allow our emotions to dictate how we feel, in turn, affecting how we respond to situations. The good news is, your Father will be waiting there to forgive you and guide you, if only you will ask. Let God into your life, fall under his authority, and allow Him to train you to become a warrior in the way you respond to life. One of my favorite Tony Robbins quotes can depict this best, "Life doesn't happen to you; it happens for you!"

Here are some verses that help me, and I hope will help you hone your ability to respond well.

"Trust in the Lord with all your heart and lean not on your own understanding; in all your ways submit to him and he will make your paths straight." Proverbs 3:5-6

"No temptation has overtaken you except what is common to mankind. And God is faithful; he will not let you be tempted beyond what you can bear. But when you are tempted, he will also provide a way out so that you can endure it." 1 Corinthians 10:13

"If any of you lacks wisdom, you should ask God, who gives generously to all without finding fault, and it will be given to you." James 1:5

Father God, thank you for helping me see where I have stepped out of obedience to your purpose for my life. Thank you for forgiving me of my choices that did not bring honor to you and the kingdom you entrusted me with. As I humbly come before you asking for forgiveness and forgiving those who have hurt me, may you grant me strength through your wisdom, to respond better to situations in my life. Father, I know that you will always show me a way to endure. May my eyes and heart be able to see that direction. May you be honored in this process of restoration, realigning my heart with yours. Thank you for giving me this day, for I am grateful to have a leader that has not lost a battle. May I allow you to lead me in all areas of my life, by humbly walking in obedience, as you have asked. I give you my heart once again, I submit to your love and authority, and may my kingdom flourish under your guidance and truth. In the name of Jesus, Amen.

The weight lifted, your heart coming back to center, know that the road from here on out will not be easy. When you choose to start walking back into obedience, the world will do all it can to stop you. Keep in mind always that your King has never lost, and already has victory waiting for you. The greatest lesson learned in my walk of obedience to God is that when we follow his words, scars heal and blessings come! That is where we are headed now, to see what is on the other side of the line we drew in the sand, the true power of obedience!

BATTLE PLAN CHAPTER 3

1. How has your heart been divided when it comes to your relationship with your Father in Heaven? How can you give that back to Him to heal and restore it?
2. Now, having a better understanding of obedience and its importance, how can you resubmit to God's authority? How are you able to give God your obedience in return for His grace?
3. As we learned, humility is important in this restoration process. How can you humble yourself to align better in obedience to God?
4. When we realign with God through obedience, we start to forgive ourselves for who we were, and take responsibility for the actions of the past, and those yet to come. How can you take responsibility for your life and move closer to who God is asking you to become?

CHAPTER FOUR

THE TRUE POWER OF OBEDIENCE

Over many years of personal development, and God working things in and out of my character, I have been able to see the fruits of obedience in my life. The greatest thing given to every one of us is our testimony. God gave us stories upon stories of men to learn from about what it looks like to be obedient and what fruits it will bear. Through the stories God has given us, we can learn how to align with his purpose for our lives, and also through a long-lost profession. Now I say "long-lost," because there are not many left in the world today. They have become big business operations, not family-owned livelihoods. This profession or occupation is farming.

Throughout civilization, farming has not only been instrumental in advancing culture and society, it was also a primary way to teach lessons of faith. Thankfully I can relate to this firsthand, as I grew up on a farm in central Wisconsin for the first 18 years of my life. For those of you who have never been on a farm or really learned about this way of life, let me take you on a journey of one year in the life of a farmer.

Before the sun rises, a man gets out of bed to clothe himself for the day. As he quietly sneaks to the mudroom, where farm clothes are stored due to smell and dirt, he can hear the cows letting him know it's time to go to work. He starts milking cows at 4:30 am and finishes around 6 am—for a farm of our size at the time. Next, it is on to feeding the animals breakfast after their labor of giving gallons of milk.

As the animals are all fed from old to young, he heads into the house to eat breakfast. From there, it is on to the many tasks that need to be done, depending on the season. Tilling the ground, planting crops, bailing hay, picking stones out of the fields, assisting with the birth of new calves, fixing equipment—if they can't they learn how cutting firewood, clearing brush, draining fields of pooled up water from the night before, so crops don't drown. The list could keep going, but you get the picture of the thousands of jobs that need to be done in the course of the day. While not all these tasks are done at once, you can see the list is extensive and has to be done in order to make it to tomorrow. Then it is back to milking cows around 4 pm, and if the sun is still up, back to the job at hand to finish a little more before dark. Finally, as the day closes, after he has served the animals, worked the ground, done odd tasks for his family, and taught his children a few lessons of life, he is able to eat dinner. End of day one!!

Now, this career path is not for the faint of heart. For the most part, there are no days off, even in the summer and winter months. You may be asking, what does this have to do with the fruit of obedience, and why you should strive to submit to God daily? Well, we need a visual to see what this looks like, at least if you are like I am. One specific example in farming, the process of growing crops, is where I want to show you the power of obedience.

TILLING THE GROUND

In order to plant crops, we must first survey the ground where we intend to plant. As farmers know, from year to year, there are better fields to plant certain crops. They must know what they want to plant and where it needs to go. So once they have determined where they are planting corn, soybeans, or hay, they then head into the shed to pull out the equipment necessary to get the ground ready.

I believe I was eleven or twelve when I really got to start helping in the field. This process, as I learned, was probably the second most important job there is when it comes to planting crops. As my dad showed me over many years of riding with him, making sure the ground was turned, the fields were smooth, and the ditches were dug for the water to drain, it would be many hours of hard work to make sure the soil was ready.

There is nothing better than getting on a tractor, the smell of power and diesel igniting the heart of a boy, to the ancient ways of sowing and reaping. There were many days I would come home so plastered in dirt, that I had to jump in the pond behind our house to get it loose enough that I could shower in the house. As I would drive around the fields making sure they were perfect, and at times wasting too much fuel, there would be moments of pride and love in a way I have never experienced. Seeing the fruits of my hours of labor, ground prepared for dad and grandpa to plant would be a lesson I could only understand later in my life.

> So many times as men in our journey through life, we forget to till the ground. We think that we can just throw seeds on hard soil, maybe water them from time to time, and boom—good crop. But we all know, and most times, after it's too late, we should have paid better attention to where we were planting seeds.

I learned through my life that the heart is the greatest field God wants to sow seeds into. We must be willing to ask tough questions of ourselves, which I believe you have done throughout the course of this book, and your life. When we give way to the painstaking labor of tilling the ground of our hearts, we can see God trying to plant a seed on that good ground.

In Pat Morely's book "How God Makes Men," he describes what God is trying to do in our hearts and through our circumstances. He says in his lesson regarding Moses' life and what we can learn from it, "...there were things God wanted to work into the character of Moses, and there were things He wanted to work out of his character, and those things take time, Bible Time."[1]

In asking God questions, which can be tough to look in the mirror, we start to till the field of our hearts so God can develop our character. God wants you to put in the work of tilling the ground, and He wants to start working into your character seeds of who He formed you to be. To help you in your labor, here are some questions, along with actions I had to take to work the field of my heart.

Q – Why is my life not turning out as I had planned?

Work – I needed to look at what was planted in my heart over time. The false expectations I imposed on myself, the expectations the world sowed into my field without my knowing, and why did I choose to fall out of obedience to the one who knew me before I was born.[2]

While the answers were not always pleasant, it allowed me to get dirty and see that God had a better way if I would only submit to it.

Q – Why am I giving God only half of the field?

Work – This question sent me on a path I did not know I needed to walk down. It sent me on a personal development overhaul. I started to read books, listen to podcasts, and watch every sermon I could find. Through this process of what I thought was wasting too much fuel, I soon discovered the answer to the question: I was afraid. I was so filled with fear that I wouldn't get what I wanted and that people may judge me. I chose to give God only the worst side of the field. Even though it was the worst in my eyes, to God, it was all he needed to show me that he wanted more of my heart. He continued to bring good crops out of bad soil which, in a farmer's world, never happens. But only through him showing me this, through my working the field and getting dirty, could he bring good fruit.

Now there are so many more actions I had to take, and questions I had to ask, in the process of getting my heart ready for what God wanted to plant. We all will have a never-ending workload in the restoration of our hearts, but take courage that while you're working the land, he is already preparing the rain.

PLANTING

As I finished one field, I could see my dad starting to plant. With precision, the seeds were set into the soil, the ground gently laid back over the seed, and each row perfectly spaced apart. When it comes to seeds, there is a variety to choose from; 60-day yield – 90-day yield – 120-day yield in regards to corn and the days it takes to become a mature crop. While most farmers shoot for the highest number of days because it allows for the best crop, it doesn't always work that way. Due to rain, lack of warm weather, lack of humidity, and many other natural issues, crops may die, and the field will have to be replanted with shorter day corn to recover at least some of the crop.[3]

In my journey to resubmit to God, He showed me that sometimes I wasn't planting the right seeds. Now, this hurts because I know I was trying my best, as most of us men do! I was reading daily and trying to put people into my life that would strengthen me and help me become who God was asking me to be. There would be days when I would try to plant good seeds of hope, love, trust, kindness, respect, and honesty, yet I was never seeing the seeds I planted come out of the ground. This is best depicted by Jesus himself in this parable:

"A farmer went out to sow seeds. While he was scattering the seed, some of it fell by the road. The birds came and ate all that seed. Other seeds fell on rocky ground, where there was not enough dirt. It grew very fast there because the soil was not deep. But when the sun rose, it burned the plants. The plants died because they did not have deep roots. Some other seeds fell among thorny weeds. The weeds grew and stopped the good plants from growing." Matthew 13:3-7

Those words hit home! I was never planting on good ground; all the good I was trying to do was being swallowed up by the world and killed because of the pressure and circumstances I was facing. This started to draw me one step closer to God because I could finally see that by my hands, these seeds were trying to grow.

> **It was by my selfish nature I wanted to be recognized for the crops growing and bearing fruit. I was planting seeds that had a short shelf life. They were for my gain and I wasn't paying attention to where they were being planted. So many of us may have the right seeds of integrity, hope, and love, but we continue to plant them in the wrong fields or areas of our life.**

Maybe this is where you are, seeing all the good you plant everywhere being taken advantage of, and you are seen as an easy meal. I know the feeling! There is hope here because you are now aware. You are now starting to see that good seed may not get planted in the right places. This is awesome news because that means you can start choosing the right place to sow those seeds. That is the direction God walked me towards. "Become obedient to who I am and what I am asking, and let me determine the harvest from the seeds you sow." Your job is just to prepare the ground and sow the seed. This removed so much pressure from having to be perfect, having to maintain the seeds I had sown, and worrying whether they would even grow. That is not our job, gentlemen! God wants you to work the land of your heart and sow good seeds into it! Then comes the fun part after you have done this work to prepare and plant—wait and keep praying.

THE WAITING GAME

Now, wait a minute, you may be asking, "How is that the fun part?" It is not! This may be the hardest part of farming and even our lives today. To wait upon the seed we have sown to produce a harvest can be very difficult, yet exactly what our Father in Heaven has been waiting for. Throughout my life, while farming and watching my family farm, I have seen our faith tested. We have had to pray for rain some days, while others we were praying the clouds would move to give us some sun, and there were even some days we just threw our hands up in the air and said we give up. Now, we never really gave up, but it was a plea for God to do what only he could, and that controlled whether the crops had what they needed to grow. Abraham's life was a great example of the waiting game. He was a man who left his home on a command God gave him, to go to a land he didn't know, was given a promise of a harvest in that he would bear a son, and then had to give up that son to show his obedience and faith to God. Here in the middle is the example, the waiting for a son after God gave the promise.

Abraham was about seventy-five years old when God told him he would have a son. The excitement in his heart had to be overwhelming even though Abraham claimed he was too old. The hope that his legacy would live on had to be coursing through his veins. Day after day, he waited, working his fields, tending to his herd, trusting in God's promise. Those days soon turned into months and those months turned into years, twenty-five years of waiting! Now crops do not take twenty-five years to grow in today's world, but to a farmer, at times, it can seem that long. This story shows us that there will be a season of relying on God to help give our seeds what they will need to grow. Please catch this: you cannot make them grow because you do not control the elements required to do so. We tend to think we can control the situations and outcomes in our lives only to see when our expectations are not met, that we should have placed God in the lead.[4]

So just like Abraham in his twenty-five years of seasons or waiting, on our farm, we would get done planting sometime in May and then we would wait to harvest in the October/November timeframe. In this season of waiting on the promise of a harvest, we needed to tend to each field.

> **While we could not make it rain, or make the sun beat down its life-giving nourishment, we could control the weeds.**

Sometimes we would spray for them to get them before they came out of the ground or when they were exceedingly small. Other times we had to take a piece of equipment and turn the soil in between the rows to make sure only the corn was taking root, and pull the weeds by hand. We tended to the seeds the best we could by making sure what could steal their nourishment was minimized or eradicated completely.

As we journey through this life, we have to remember the seeds of truth, love, honesty, integrity, stewardship, humility, and honor. We must tend to the weeds of sin and lies in our lives, and those lies of the world that are competing for this precious space God is trying to cultivate something in. Our obedience to the work of pulling the weeds out of our hearts will soon bring a harvest that we cannot imagine. Stay patient in the promise that God knows what you need! Yet the length of time required in growing that seed is on Bible Time, not our concept or expectation of how long it should take. This will test your faith over and over, but any farmer will tell you the feeling of accomplishment during harvest will far outweigh the struggles of the waiting game!

HARVEST TIME

Now the reward to your obedience and its true power. As you have tended to your heart, and have seen mini harvests along the way in your patience and endurance, we must head out now to collect the main harvest. To add to the fruit of your obedience, let's finish what Jesus said in Matthew regarding good seed.

"Still other seed fell on good soil, where it produced a crop—a hundred, sixty or thirty times what was sown." Matthew 13:8

Each kernel of corn that is planted in the ground will bring a stalk that will potentially yield, depending on the growing conditions, 2 to 4 ears of corn. Each ear carries anywhere between 500 to 1,200 kernels of corn on them![5] The farmer knows the reward for his hours of obedience, and days of exhaustion, long periods of no rain, or too much rain, days questioning whether or not he did all he could.

While he doesn't know the exact yield, he leans on the promise above, that his work will produce a crop so abundant that it will fill the storehouses of his needs for the seasons that are around the corner. This harvest will feed his animals, provide income to the household for many months, allowing him to keep the lights on and send his kids to school. You see, we must wait in patient, joyful expectation for the harvest God promises through our obedience.

Gentlemen, God wants to show you his grace and favor by staying the course. Stay under his command, heed his words, because he wants to give you what you cannot even see.

> **As those seeds grow in our lives, God is tending to them. We may not understand at times how much we will reap when we sow, but we will always get a harvest. Let's just make sure we are sowing good seed, in good soil, in the right season, so the only one who can make it grow has good ground to work with.**

KNOW YOUR SEASONS

To even get through the process of tilling up the ground, sowing seeds, tending to the fields, and harvesting, we need to be obedient to the season of our lives. A farmer knows that he cannot plant corn in December because the ground will be frozen, and the corn will die. He also knows that he cannot start mid-summer because the crop will not mature in time to maximize its yield. When we are obedient to God, we can recognize more clearly the seasons we are in. We can see that we should not try to harvest before we plant, we cannot leave our hearts unattended because weeds will take over, we cannot neglect our family because of our selfish ambitions, we cannot receive something that we have not worked for. This does not mean that God will not bless you earlier than expected or give you what you need before you ask. He is God and will do as he sees fit.

What I want you to see is that your obedience in each season will have its reward. King Solomon, regarded as the wisest man that ever lived, knew this when he said

"There is a time for everything, and a season for every activity under the heavens:

A time to be born and a time to die,

A time to plant and a time to uproot,

A time to kill and a time to heal,

A time to tear down and a time to build,

A time to weep and a time to laugh,

A time to mourn and a time to dance,

A time to scatter stones and a time to gather them,

A time to embrace and a time to refrain from embracing,

A time to search and a time to give up,
A time to keep and a time to throw away,
A time to tear and a time to mend,
A time to be silent and a time to speak,
A time to love and a time to hate,
A time for war and a time for peace."[5]

There is so much here that could probably be written in another book! My point in sharing this scripture is to show you the wisdom in knowing these seasons. Each season, you will be tested to see where your obedience lies. Will you be patient as you submit to the one who knows your season? Will you find peace in knowing he will bring about a harvest? Can you give your best with the expectation that God knows what you need even when you don't?

Solomon goes on to say that God has made everything beautiful in its time and that we cannot fathom what God has truly done from beginning to end. He then makes a statement that I hope you will find peace and reassurance in. He says that God will make sure your obedience is rewarded. It shows you God's heart towards us and how we use the seasons to glorify him. "I know that there is nothing better for people than to be happy and to do good while they live. That each of them may eat and drink and find satisfaction in all their toil—this is the gift of God."[6]

Can you see it now? God is trying to give you a gift, a harvest for your obedience to work the fields of your heart and kingdom. He wants you to eat, and drink, and find satisfaction with your toil! True obedience brings power to your life that only a gracious Father can give. We must learn to steward this opportunity to work in the right seasons well, so that the harvest can give Him glory, and keep us on the path of becoming who he has called us to be.

My grandfather was one of the greatest men I have ever known. He represented this process so well, and sadly I did not learn this lesson until he had passed. While reflecting on the life of a great man who, through his obedience to the fields God gave him to work, raised an amazing family. The impact he has had on all of us will span generations to come. He was a man who was rarely startled, always had an answer, found a level of peace I wanted to attain and lived with an integrity that I have never seen before. He was a farmer, father, and friend. On my plane ride back from the funeral, I recalled so many things he would tell us. You know, Grandpa wisdom. Later in his life, I remember asking him how he had been married for so long, and how he always stayed in this place of peace? His answer finally made sense, "Well, it's actually pretty simple," he said.

"You remember all the times I put up the Christmas lights for Grandma? I chose to do that so she would be happy. When the cows needed to be milked before the sun rose, when the ice cream machine broke at 1 am, when the fields needed to be worked, I knew that I had two options. Either complain and grumble that these things needed to be done, or make a choice to do them, because then I was in control of what I chose to do."

Choice! How my grandfather stayed obedient to his work and his family came from his power to choose! Perspective!

He lived from this place that he could make change even if he did not feel like it, because he was given responsibility and power to be a good steward. He did not leave it up to chance or luck. His alignment came from God's greatest gift in our lives, the power to choose what we will do, how we will do it, and who we will do it for.

Before we dig into this gift, take some time to reflect on the power of obedience, by tending to what God has given you. May this prayer help unlock the power of obedience in your life and bring you peace to run your race, the way only you can!

Father God, thank you for showing me that there are seasons in which my obedience matters. Thank you for showing me your power through your son Jesus, and his promises of yielding more than we have sown. May the seeds I plant be of great joy to you, and honor you, as you give them the provision needed to bring about a harvest. As a farmer works his land, may I also work the areas of my heart, so that you can have room to bring about change, love, and peace. May I lean on your power and provision by submitting to your love and grace, through simply working what you have given me to the best of my ability. I know I cannot see what abundance will be coming, but you do! So Father help cover me with your strength and wisdom as I serve you with my whole heart and honor you through heeding your commands. Please bless my kingdom with your love, and may my obedience make you smile. Thank you for showing me your power and the way to walk in that power. In Jesus' name, Amen!

BATTLE PLAN CHAPTER 4

1. We know in the journey of restoration we must learn to work the fields of our heart. What are 2-3 areas in your heart you can work on? How can you give these areas to God as well?
2. When we till the ground of our hearts and put good things in, we must then plant good seeds and let God help them grow. How can you give God the good seeds you're sowing so he can help you produce a harvest?
3. Staying patient as you do good and work hard is definitely no easy task. What are some things or bible verses you can use to help you stay patient and wait upon the Lord in obedience?
4. Recognizing the season we are in is vital to where our work fits in relation to God's work. What season are you in? What needs to be done in your heart in this season to help you stay aligned with God's will for your life?

PART THREE

MATTERS OF THE HEART

CHAPTER FIVE

HOW DO WE BRIDGE THE GAP?

We are at a critical stage in our journey. To get from where we are on this island of the past, disobedience, and a heart that was never really relying on God to hold it, we must bridge the gap. This gap may be bigger for some than others, depending on where you are in your journey with God. Personally, I felt that the canyon I had to cross was more like going from the United States to Europe. But remember, God is never far away, always standing with us in struggle and success. This is best depicted in the story of the prodigal son. When the young man who turned away for a time came back to his father, his father ran to meet him. God, right here, right now, is running after you like you're running to Him.[1] Trust in that as you take a step of great faith and courage. The gap from where you are, to where God wants you to go, can only be crossed with a bridge. That bridge is CHOICE. Just like the lesson my grandfather taught me by the way he lived his life, choice brings obedience and sacrifice into alignment. To understand how obedience and sacrifice play a big role in our choices, we need to know how a bridge works.

"They do it by carefully balancing two main kinds of forces called **compression** (a pushing or squeezing force, acting inward) and **tension** (a pulling or stretching force, acting outward), channeling the **load** (the total weight of the bridge and the things it carries) onto **abutments** (the supports at either side) and **piers** (one or more supports in the middle). Although there are many kinds of bridges, virtually all of them work by balancing compressive forces in some places with tensile forces elsewhere, so there's no *overall* force to cause motion and do damage."[2]

In this explanation, you see that a bridge can only stand by the balancing of two forces, compressive and tensile. They must be in perfect harmony for the bridge to maintain its integrity and carry the loads it was designed to carry.

Our choices are no different. When we align our choices with the compressive force inwardly in obedience while making the right outwardly or tensile force of sacrifice, the strength of our walk is now made to carry the purpose God has predestined for us. One without the other, and your bridge will crumble.

OBEDIENCE vs. SACRIFICE

Through my journey, I have come to see that there are three main choices God wants us to make on our walk with him through this life. In each of these areas, we will break down what it looks like to have obedience and sacrifice working together to solidify our choices in building a life that gives God all the glory.

THE BRIDGE OF UNITY

Our entire existence has been a disunity between our Father and fellow man. In the Garden of Eden, when Adam chose to eat what God asked him not to, disunity filled our bloodline. Ever since that day, God has been working to restore unity to every person through His son, Jesus. We look at Adam's choice first, and we can see that obedience and sacrifice were not in perfect balance. That choice sent the balance of these two heavenly forces spiraling downward for thousands of years. Nation on top of nation fought to eliminate the other. Men sought power and control apart from God. They chose to make sacrifices instead of being obedient, which in turn cost them their lives and the prosperity of generations to come.

When I think of disunity and the problem it creates, my heart hurts. Not only from my experiences, but also for God. Jesus was His son, and the only way to bring unity to his creation was to allow him to become flesh and die. God chose disunity in Heaven, to restore unity on earth, by sending Jesus. Now, he knew the rest of the story before we did. He would restore His son and all of us, but I believe it's worth noting the price. God was obedient to his word and promise, and that choice required a perfect sacrifice to restore unity between heaven and earth. Being a father myself, I cannot imagine sending my daughter to die for the wrongs of the people I created. Yet let me tell you how thankful I am that he did. As I have walked away from God, like so many of us have at different points in our lives, it's amazing to know that we still have a path to unity with our heavenly father along with our fellow man.

Strife, anger, hatred, malice, judging, lies, and selfishness all follow disunity. In building a better choice through Unity, we must understand what will be required of each of us, to make this bridge carry the load it's designed to carry. Unity, in its greatest form, has brought armies together to win great victories, restored marriages, brought parent and child back together, and has removed bitterness from the hearts of men for centuries. You can look at any civilization and see where unity has been both good and bad, where sacrifices were made to kill millions in obedience to a false God, religion, or ideology. On the other hand, you can see where it has restored humanity to the true glory in which it was created.

As you tend to the fields of your heart and kingdom, we must make choices of unity to bring our kingdom together. Here are some ways that through the choice of unity, you can see how obedience and sacrifice are balanced to bring peace.

FAMILY, WORK, RELATIONSHIPS

When a husband makes a choice to bring unity to his family, he looks to seek harmony. He will be obedient to his wife by staying committed to her physically, spiritually, and emotionally. He will sacrifice time at a bar with buddies, because the environment is not being conducive to keeping his eyes from wandering. He will choose to pray for his wife and children in obedience to be their protector and leader. This will cause him to sacrifice selfish prayers for his needs and wants to align as a servant to his family. In the unseen when a man chooses to consciously look at a situation within his family to bring unity, hope, and grace—God finally has a canvas He can work on. This canvas is created because you are willing to be obedient to Him and sacrifice your time, energy, and emotions for the betterment of your family.

Now while we can see these are simple choices on the outside, inside every man, in different capacities, they are wars. Internally, evil wants to plant seeds that will grow into hedgerows, dividing your heart from God.

> **The battle here is to come before God, and see that you can win if you relinquish control to a God that already knows your struggle. Here He will honor your obedience because of the sacrifice of His Son, and give you a way to defeat what is trying to create disunity.**

We also know that Jesus came to divide, to separate believers from unbelievers. He came as a double-edged sword.[3] This should tell us that sometimes in our families, when we seek unity, it can only come through separation. This may look like keeping some family at a distance in your life because they are unhealthy towards you and your kingdom. The obedience to leading your family well will require the good sacrifice of making choices to cut ties with family members who do not have your best interest at heart. This will bring pain, regret, and even hostility. We as men must be willing to carry these sacrifices with our heavenly Father, to protect the kingdom He has entrusted to our care.

When obedience and sacrifice are out of balance regarding unity, we see that sides are taken within our family. Wives do not respect their husbands; husbands do not love their wives. Our parents become more important than those living under our own roof. Children may become the center of the relationship, which drives husband and wife apart because they sacrifice their unity to become obedient to the needs of a child. While it's important to take care of your children as God takes care of us, the union of husband and wife with God will represent more to that child than becoming obedient to them. When they see mom and dad taking date nights, helping each other with responsibility, praying for each other, it shows them that there is strength in obedience to their choice. That the sacrifice of finding time to continually date, working as a unit, and putting the other first will bring more fruit in the long run than getting what they want today.

Now, if you're single and understand that the above examples are what you want to have in your home, start practicing them now. We get what we are! If you want to have unity with your future spouse, date her with that action in mind. This will require you to sacrifice the fleshly desires you have before you're married. For example, don't move in together before you're married. Instead, sacrifice what you want, to actually learn the heart of the person you are dating. These sacrifices and more are in obedience to your choice to someday be unified with your future spouse and kids.

Unity is a powerful choice God gave each of us. To bring us home to him, He gave us his son. Abraham wanted unity with God, so he was willing to move and give up his son Isaac.[4] David sought unity through always coming to God in praise and repentance.[5] Solomon sought unity with God by honoring his father and asking for wisdom instead of wealth and power.[6] Each man in the Bible who ever accomplished anything God wanted us to learn, was done through a choice of unity.

First to God, then to the kingdom they were given. The obedience to that choice required a sacrifice of ego, pride, wealth, homes, and security. Yet the rewards for that balance brought Israel out of Egypt,[7] helped Nehemiah build a wall to protect God's people,[8] raised Lazarus from the dead,[9] and helped Peter walk on water.[10] Each of us has a place in our hearts that we can never fill. That place is unity with our Father, through a life of obedience to his command, and sacrifices of our selfish, fleshly desires. This is a daily choice that will enrich your days in a way only God can.

"I appeal to you, brothers and sisters, in the name of our Lord Jesus Christ, that all of you agree with one another in what you say and that there be no divisions among you, but that you be perfectly united in mind and thought." 1 Corinthians 1:10

"Bear with each other and forgive one another if any of you has a grievance against someone. Forgive as the Lord forgave you. And over all these virtues put on love, which binds them all together in perfect unity." Colossians 3:13-14

BRIDGE OF HUMILITY

We all love to have our egos stroked, and know that we are worth something to the world. While this can be good, one of the most rewarding things we can do as men is to learn the art of humility. It is a choice that will take much effort and awareness, to keep the forces of sacrifice and obedience working in harmony. Bringing humility was something God did regularly in the old testament. He chose to humble a people that would not honor him, and only him. We do the same with our children, or maybe that happens when we try and play a sport we used to be good at, then 20 years later must be humbled because our bodies cannot keep up. There are only two ways to look at humility. Either you choose to be humble, or God will make you humble. I have learned that this can be difficult on a day-to-day basis. With mounting pressures to perform at work, while leading your family, being looked to for all the answers, in searching to belong, we fluff up who we used to be, instead of being who we are. These pressures, or bad seeds, lead to an abundance of wrong sacrifice, and disobedience to whom God is asking us to be. The bridge then begins to falter. Our worth is caught up in what we think we know, and who we used to be. Well, maybe even who we have become if you have any success in your life today. While you should never limit what you can give to others from your success, a humble heart will always keep you grounded.

When we choose humility, obedience becomes easier, because we know we are only grains of sand. Sacrifices though, may get harder, at least internally. Can you imagine what the disciples thought about Jesus when he humbled himself before them and washed their feet? I picture myself there and start to get extremely uncomfortable. Looking at my brothers, I say He has healed so many and is royalty, why is he doing such a thing. Then I try to get on my knees and wash the feet of my friends and family, just as Jesus did.[11] Here it's where I see the love and expression of obedience carry much force in the kingdom's decision of humility. The outward reflection and sacrifice to Jesus's image, for most of us, is a sacrifice we are unwilling to make. Yet when Jesus sacrificed this so-called image of who people thought he was, to become obedient to his purpose, no one can deny the power of humility, and respect that was earned. It was an example to show us that the first will be last and the last will be first. Jesus showed us that the decision to humble ourselves will bring rewards first internally and then externally.

Within our walk as men, we must also see humility from a place of wisdom. My grandfather always read the paper! We could ask him any current event question and he knew the answer. I once watched him and his brother finish a crossword puzzle in under 10 minutes. Yet, he would always tell us that true wisdom came from knowing what you do not know. When you get to the place of humility in learning, you see that there is nothing but upside. This shows that you can remove your ego and arrogance because you have the opportunity to learn. Solomon may be the best example of this ever! God wanted us to see that when we humbly come before him and seek only God's discernment, the other desires of our heart are added to our life.[12]

I recall a time this was very evident in my life. As the day neared for my wedding, we were solidifying plans for our honeymoon. I chose this time around to ask God for his discernment to lead my family well. That he would always guide me, and focused on staying as humble as possible. The rewards for this humility came in the form of, a bonus from work, a honeymoon in Hawaii, and the news a baby was on the way. While there may be more that leads into each of these blessings, looking back, it was when I was most humble, that I received the most internally and externally from God. It's not Solomon's life, but we all know that when we are humble, we grow. Sacrificing here for your ego and your obedience to purpose suffers. Good sacrifice and humbling ourselves will always bring obedience to one greater than we are. It rewards our family and friends with love, patience, wisdom, and a servant leader. We must pursue humility with the right heart to show our obedience to the gift we have been given. This allows our sacrifices to carry weight words cannot describe. Choose to humble yourself, before God needs to step in and humble you; as we all know that is never enjoyable.

When you choose to be humble, the power of obedience and sacrifice become stronger than at any other point, because you are not in control. God tells us to humble ourselves. To become less, so that he can be more in our lives. There is wisdom here that I cannot stress enough, as I myself have learned, and maybe you have too. When we walk in humility, serve in humility, love with humility, we are like little children getting to have fun all over again.

> **If there is anything you gain from this chapter, may it be that in humbling yourself by choice, God becomes the stabilizer between obedience and sacrifice. Which in turn, eases the burden of your heart and brings a harvest that only he can bring.**

"For all those who exalt themselves will be humbled, and those who humble themselves will be exalted." Luke 14:11

"Humble yourselves, therefore, under God's mighty hand, that he may lift you up in due time." 1 Peter 5:6

BRIDGE OF HONOR

My wife and I went to Oahu for our honeymoon. Trying to take everything in, a tour to Pearl Harbor was a must. As we floated above the ship graveyard in the harbor, my heart began to ache. Tears started to form as the immense feeling of what happened overcame me. To think that thousands of men lost their lives in the bombings of Pearl Harbor and were locked in ships below us was beyond humbling. Docking at the Arizona memorial, we were directed to keep quiet. The silence here was not only taken very seriously, but it showed a sign of respect to those who lost their lives that day. We walked up the ramp and into the memorial; here you see the names of so many who died, so that we may live. Oil trickled out from underneath us and floated away in the harbor. That oil symbolized the cries of those lost at sea—one of the greatest representations of honor I have ever seen in my life.

Having many men in my life who fought for my freedom, this bridge is one we must never forget. Not only because military men and women have fought and died for the rights that we so lavishly enjoy, but generations before us have done the same. Maybe you had alcoholism that ran in your family for generations, and your grandfather or father ended that battle through obedience to a better future, and the sacrifice of the flesh. Maybe divorce has plagued your family for generations and your parents were the only ones who chose to stop that disease. Maybe you are the only Christian in your family and the battle you're fighting for is for the generations not yet born.

Every man's life that has come before us must be honored. God saw fit to leave us the genealogy of his creation, so that we may honor him, and the lives of those who came before us.

> **We must honor their struggles. We must honor their courage. We must honor the God who helped give them a way through the valley to bring us victory. Honoring those who have fought hard brings humility to our lives. It also brings obedience and sacrifice into a vessel that can be shared.**

It is here that we appreciate life by learning from those sacrifices that were made for us, and where their obedience lay—we see a roadmap marked with great paths and hazards.

Choosing to honor someone is an act of obedience to their life, and a sacrifice of our time and energy to learn from their life. This was especially important to our Heavenly Father, so much so that he put it on tablets called the ten commandments. He wrote, "you shall have no other gods beside me, honor your father and mother, honor your neighbor!"[13] Paul came after and said more of the same, that we must honor each other in servitude, gentleness, humility, and love.[14] Honor would be the foundational choice to align with the power of our Heavenly Father. It is in this place we have no choice but to humble ourselves and seek unity to gain wisdom.

The good sacrifices that come from honoring others is a change in behavior followed by obedience to God, who showed you a new way. This Bridge of Honor allows us to reflect and appreciate all God has done and revealed to us. For none of us can fathom what God has done from beginning to end. It is in honor we see his power and love. Here is where we learn to honor our struggles for what they are doing to our character. Patrick Morley says it well in his book How God Makes Men. He tells us an important lesson God wants us to learn in honoring Moses' life, "God makes men by taking us through a humbling process that fundamentally changes the way we think."[15] When we honor others and even our struggles, we cannot help but be humbled by an amazing Father who not only corrects us but forgives and blesses!

Your obedience in taking the time to remember those who have come before you, and honoring their sacrifices, will bring wisdom and reward that paves the way for the next generation. We see that in each of these choices, God wants to redeem us, the way we think, and how we show up in our kingdoms. To decide daily to filter our choices in these three areas, we gain a heavenly strength to align the forces of obedience and sacrifice. We take courage in this because as God has made the same three choices, we too, can now walk in the footsteps of our Father. Remember, the road will not be easy, but it will reward you, and generations to come, with an example of the love your Heavenly Father gave you.

Do you feel empowered? Seeing the world for what it is, learning what good and bad sacrifices are! Seeing that your obedience is more powerful than anything you can give to God. Understanding that what you sow and tend to in your heart and kingdom matters! To know that you have learned how to harness the true alignment and understanding of two powerful forces given to us by our Heavenly Father. We can see how this alignment takes center stage in every lesson we learn. When I started to understand this way of thinking, each book I read in the Bible, and by other men, carried different wisdom to it now. Making their words carry more meaning because I could honor them in their obedience and struggle, as well as see how God wanted to teach me from their lives.

As you are gaining momentum and understanding, remember to stay patient, as well as put on the armor God has given you.[16] With every level of our journey, the tests become tougher, the lessons harder to learn, yet the rewards of our faith come in abundance. As you already know, when you choose to live for Christ, life does not always go easy or as planned. Yet, we can take courage in knowing that we are not alone. You have worked the fields of your heart and built better bridges to honor God with your life through choice. The next stop is kingdom expansion! As you journey into new territory, it will come with new blessings and new battles.

BATTLE PLAN CHAPTER 5

1. What are some choices you can make that, with the right amount of obedience and sacrifice, that God can use to bless you and others in your kingdom?
2. The bridges or choices of Unity, Humility, and Honor, can create a powerful force in our lives when we use them well. How can you continually keep these choices at the forefront of your mind?
3. In what areas of your life can you implement these three bridges to become more obedient to God's heart and will for your kingdom?
4. We see with the right obedience and the right sacrifice, our choices withstand the storms of life. This is a skill learned over time, with the help of our Father, and obedience to His word. As you learn this new skill of making better choices, who is someone you can help along the way in your journey? Whom can you reach out to, and share your choices with, to help keep you accountable?

CHAPTER SIX

NEW TERRITORY

Just after landing in Tampa from the long flight from my honeymoon, I was overwhelmed with a sense of compassion. We were able to see so much beauty in Hawaii, the kind you never forget. Honoring the memories we had just made together to start our marriage, the sunsets we witnessed, and the majesty of how God makes mountains and streams in the middle of the ocean. Deep within me, there was a part that welled up, this sense of now it's your turn. I was not sure what that meant until a couple of months later. We passed through Christmas, and I knew that my brother-in-law and his wife were having some issues. I felt God say it again, "It's time to step up and love as I have loved you." So, I called Tim and decided to love him no matter what he was going through. The first step in this new territory of serving with my whole heart, as God asked, was to seek the heart of Tim.

We set out to do just that. I knew of him through family gatherings, what sports he loved, his love for his wife and daughter, how hard he worked, and how he loved to serve others. Yet like most of us men, these things are only the exterior of a man. To love fully as God asks, we must venture out and explore the new territory God is asking us to go through.

Tim and I met at a local restaurant for about 2 hours. Here is where I stepped out in utter faith, to truly learn the history of one of my best friends and brother in Christ. This was new territory for me because it was not for personal gain, our meeting wasn't a stepping stone to fix Tim's marriage, and it definitely wasn't so I could fix his past. I learned long ago that to honor another brother in arms, we must be willing to walk through their story with them. This allows us to see what has shaped them. It shows us where God stepped in and loved them, when they could not love themselves. Being so excited, we ordered some appetizers and dug in. Tim proceeded to tell me his upbringing, what struggles he faced throughout his life, that his wife Vanessa had saved him from the depths of despair, and that he never really had brothers that stepped in to truly love him.

Now please understand the people who stepped in were those of his mixed martial arts life. He loved them passionately because they loved him for who he was. Yet as we all sometimes know, when we leave those competitive families, we see we must learn to fight alone, or find another family for a fight with. He was an amazing MMA fighter in his short career. When Tim left MMA, he lost part of who he was. I could see in his eyes his heart longing for a family like that again. Not a family that would replace his current wife and daughter, but a family of brothers that would push him, fight for him, and protect him at all costs. I knew this feeling all too well in my life. Never having real brothers that knew your deepest darkest secrets, brothers that would pray for you, brothers that would step in and teach you how to be a better man, and a family that could raise you to another level. I, just like Tim, am beyond thankful for those in my life. We sometimes though, feel like a piece is missing. When we walk into new territories, we almost feel overwhelmed with fear of not knowing. We are excited to push forward yet afraid of what is over the next mountain or under the next bridge we must cross.

As we ended our night, I remember Tim looking at me and saying, "Thank you brother for letting me tell you my story! Thank you for taking the time to love me and meet me where I am!" These words are forever etched into my heart! They not only remind me of Tim, but they also remind me of my Father in heaven. Those words were me saying the same thing to God. "Thank you, Lord, for meeting me where I am and knowing everything about me!" When we walk into new territory with a new heart, God shows us more of himself than we ever knew before. It was after this dinner that I looked up to the Heavens and told God I was all in. I was all in on the new territory you are asking me to journey through. This new territory was men's ministry, helping other men like myself find a friendship and love that can only come from another man. After this evening, God showed me how important it was that we fight for friendship, fight for our brothers, and build a bigger army for our Father in heaven.

LEARNING AS YOU'RE EXPLORING

As Tim and I continued to grow together, God continued to show up in my life. Just like so many of us, when we walk in the lane that God gives us, we can see him everywhere. From day to day, it varies our responsibilities as we tend to the kingdom of our hearts and lives, pressing on to new territory where we are called to help others build their kingdoms. We are called to build alliances with our brothers to form stronger kingdoms. When you step in to help someone build their kingdom through love and friendship, God steps in and shows you how he will honor your choice. He will help you resolve disagreements, he will show you how to work in unison for his kingdom, he will show you, as you connect to his word, how to sharpen each other for the battles ahead.

This is where we need to understand that with new territory comes new responsibility. We are now not only responsible for our kingdom, and it's ever so important not to neglect it, but we are responsible for helping in the expansion and protection of our brother's kingdom. Now we cannot tell them how to build their kingdom, but we can walk alongside them as they succeed and fail, just as we have. Sometimes it's not about fixing; it's about knowing you're not alone through trials and success.

When you choose to expand your kingdom and help others, there are now new sacrifices that will need to be made. Yet what you are obedient to must stay grounded in your Heavenly Father! I remember what it's like to look at someone else's life and say to myself, "I wish I had what they have…" Dangerous! As we journey through this new territory, we must remember what got us here—our obedience to God, and honoring him through our sacrifices.

> **Looking only at the outside of others' lives is dangerous, because you do not know what they have been through.**

Therefore, it's very important to learn the true heart of your brother so that you can appreciate the struggles and work put into his walk. Where God has shown him the rewards and failures of his obedience and sacrifice, in this place of humility, we see God working in our brothers, just like He is us! That whatever the outside of his kingdom looks like, his heart mimics ours.

My advice to you is, as you head into this new territory, stay consistent in what helped you build your kingdom. You have learned how to discern between right and wrong sacrifice, obedience, and disobedience, and how your choices helped you move to new places. It is crucial to stay grounded and keep learning as we move throughout this journey, for we can easily become misaligned with God's heart because of our selfishness. Below are some ways that you can stay aligned in your new journey.

1. Always seek knowledge

Here is where we are continually asking questions that have meaning. Are we talking to our brothers about real issues? Are we asking how they fight these battles? Are we leaning on them to pray for us when we fall short? Are we spending time with each other to not only learn about each other's hearts but also to bring relief to our hearts through laughter and mindless banter? Are you seeking God's wisdom together? Are you learning from the decisions you made and how God wants you to become better?

2. Always humble yourself in the process

Are you arrogant, boasting of your success? Are you neglecting your own kingdom or allowing God to multiply your obedience? Are you learning from your brothers because you want to know them better or just to hear them talk so you can have a turn? Are you paying attention to your heart when others win? Humility in our new territory will allow God to bring us together faster and stronger. There is wisdom to be found in humble relationships.

3. Always build new bridges

I cannot stress enough how your choices will matter in this new land. Learn from where you have come from, honor the struggles that God used to shape you, then make choices to help others cross into new territories. It is not in finishing on the top of the mountain alone that we have a life well-lived. You cannot climb Everest alone; you will perish. You must choose your running mates well, become obedient to the God who wants an army of one, and then make sacrifices for each other to advance up the mountain as a single unit. Your choice to move ahead without your brothers will cause you to sacrifice friendship for success, humility for ego, and love for pride. Yet, if each of us as men come together as a single unit obedient to God, our sacrifices will bring glory to Him, for He will lead us well.

NEW BLESSINGS

When God sees that you have aligned with Him once again, that you are honoring him through your choices and alignment, amazing things start to happen. As Tim and I grew closer together, we both could see how God was moving in our lives. We could see that our families were coming closer together, our 9-5 jobs were starting to get in a better place, the impact we were making outside of our kingdom was becoming very apparent. I remember Tim telling me a story about some of his buddies at work. There was a group of men that came in one day. They were struggling, and not having the best of mornings. As they started their day, something within Tim told him to be a light to these men. So he did what he does best, he became the class clown to lift their spirits. He started asking each one what they were struggling with and walked alongside them, even for a moment to ease their burden. He would turn up the music and dance even though his dancing was more of a stiff fighter wiggle. The men rallied around this light-heartedness, and their day changed.

It's moments like this he would share, and we would laugh and talk about what it meant for him and me to have this friendship, this love of brothers. This spilled into my kingdom as well because I was more focused on finding ways to love and serve, than the issues I faced alone every day. We all know how hard it can be to fight alone, to allow the world to start to suffocate us.

> **The answer is in the blessing of finding another King, another man to fight with. It gives us perspective, and someone to walk in obedience with.**

Though the sacrifices look different because of their kingdom and situation, our obedience to loving each other and our Heavenly Father brings light to this world that cannot be snuffed out. This new territory of friendship, learning, and exploring affords us the gift of perspective. The blessing does not necessarily come in material things. Sometimes it comes in the ability to see your life in a new light. I will not downplay for one moment what you may be going through! Tim and I would attest that while you're in the thick of the fight, you cannot see the blessings around you with eyes of gratitude. Yet this does not give us the reason to give up on the hope of a better day. To dig into this new blessing, that is exactly what we did. We found gratitude. Every day for over a month, we would text each other three things we were grateful for, once before bed, and again first thing in the morning. The blessings that came from this were boundless. Tim would say it helped him look to the day with optimism, that it was a reminder of how much God had blessed him, and that no matter the storm he would have to face that day—God was going to use him.

I would mimic this blessing! My life changed because I chose to be obedient to what God asked me to do—be a light to another. Because I chose to honor God and fight for another man, to walk alongside him as men had done for me, God blessed me with my purpose. He renewed my hope that everything I had gone through in my life was leading up to fighting for other men. My relationship with my wife blossomed, as we were talking about God's plans for us more than ever. We were expecting during this time and we could see God moving in the pregnancy. Tim walked alongside Heather and I, was praying for both of us, praying over the baby, and always bringing words of hope. I will always remember God's love and light through Tim telling Heather she was always glowing during her pregnancy.

We do not understand the impact and blessings in our lives of new kingdoms and the kings that rule them, until we build bridges to walk among new territories. There are so many stories of men in the bible to give us hope as we explore new kingdoms and the blessings that come from that obedience. Abraham left his home and moved to a new kingdom, the blessing was abundance and a son.[1] Moses left his kingdom Egypt due to murder and fear of death—he met God in the desert and returned to set Israel free.[2] Joseph was sold into slavery, put into prison, and yet saved a nation from famine—even his own family.[3] David left his flock of sheep to check on his brothers and walked onto a battlefield to defeat a giant.[4] Gideon felt worthless and small. He left his kingdom, the threshing room, and assembled 300 men to defeat hundreds of thousands.[5]

> **When you walk in obedience to what God is asking you to do, blessings may not come immediately, but God is faithful to his word and will use you and the provision he gives you, to change another kingdom.**

He will also let that new territory change you. Be patient as you learn how to navigate new places. You will fail, have grace with yourself, because God does. This is one of the most exciting places we as men can get to. A place where our hearts are aligned with God, we are obedient to his words, and we make good sacrifices that honor him. Our world matches heaven in its fluidity and peace. I honestly believe this is a place we must strive to stay in, even when the storm we are about to face will require more from us than we think we can bear.

NEW BATTLES

It was a strange week in this new territory of serving Tim with my whole heart. We were not in as good of communication as we had been over the last couple of months. I knew Tim was battling some ugly things in his life, but had no idea how much he was losing the battle. As the week drew to a close, I had not heard much from him. Many thoughts go racing through our heads when we do not hear from our brothers. We do not know if they are struggling or doing well. Do they need our help and battle experience or have they marched on to a new battle? As Friday came and went there was something unsettling in my heart. Not being able to put my finger on it, I resolved to head to his house in the morning to workout, learn some boxing techniques, and smack a tire with a sledgehammer.

As I arose Saturday morning, my life changed forever. What I am about to tell you takes all the strength I have to write these words and tell you this story. It was around 6 am when I looked at my phone and saw a couple of missed calls and a text message. I always told Tim that if he ever needed me, I would be there. His text said, "I need your help!" My heart sank! This message came in the middle of the night, and my heart broke. Fear rushed through my body. What happened? What did he do? Now to help you understand where I was at, you need to know that six years earlier, Tim tried to commit suicide. He was unsuccessful and God changed his life. His beautiful wife saved him through her love and sternness. While his life got better, that evil locked within him was still a battle he fought daily.

I knew he was fighting these things amidst his marriage problems, his work issues, his finding purpose and meaning in this life. I headed to their house where I sat outside. Both cars were in the driveway. No damage! At this point, I tried to call his phone, but it went to voicemail. The hopeful part of me imagined he just passed out and forgot to plug in his phone, which was not uncommon. Pulling up the note app on my phone, I wrote down five things I would bring up to Tim, to help him and me get closer, but also help him fight his battles. I prayed to God asking Him to soften Tim's heart for the message I wanted to give him when he woke up. I headed home and was changing my clothes when the phone call came. Heather's face dropped as she heard something no one should ever have to hear, "He is cold and we don't think he is with us anymore!"

I got Heather in the car and we raced to their house. In my heart, I already knew the outcome, as we drove way too fast! The only thought I had was to get there, and be there for this family! We parked, and rushed into the house in one last hope-filled moment that we could save him. I asked everyone to get outside, and headed to the bedroom. The officers there couldn't get the door open as he was propped against it. I began trying to help free the door to save my brother, then suddenly, he lay there at my feet. The way they looked at me, confirmed what I already knew. He was gone. At that moment, I saw two forces in this world.

I saw how hard, evil, painful, and real the battles we fight are. Satan showed me what would happen when I tried to love and help another man. That walking into this new territory would carry a price that I should choose not to pay again. He tried everything he could to stop me cold in my tracks. To hinder all the progress God had made in my life, by taking away from me the one thing I went all-in on in my life. The one man I chose to give to God and love harder than I ever had. As these tears run down my face even now, retelling this moment to you, there is a peace in my heart from the second force.

This second force was God telling me Tim was now at peace. That he fought harder than anyone expected. That Jesus loved him and Tim was now home. The peace only the Holy Spirit can bring rushed over my body. These next words are what still drives me in a way I cannot describe. I felt the Spirit say, "Dustan, you have a choice!" "You can either walk away and run back to your kingdom of safety or you can fight. You can let this moment be etched into your heart forever, and build a bigger army. That choice is only yours!" I chose to be a light in this crisis. I called his family, helped take care of funeral arrangements, and fought to love each family member.

I do not say this to look like a hero. I say this because God gets all the glory in this battle. Without his strength and all the work he did in my life to prepare me, I would have been a coward and ran! It was only by staying lockstep with Him, and the men in my life, that I and all of Tim's family could heal, hour by hour, day by day. I remember calling my brothers to tell them what happened. There are two men who have always been my rock, Kyle and Bryant. Bryant knew Tim from our wedding and through me asking for prayer on behalf of Tim. He was a rock and let me show my pain and weakness, as he loved me through every day after this tragic loss. Kyle and I were on the phone; though he did not know Tim, he knows me better than anyone else. His words to me will forever keep me fighting. "Be a light and build a bigger army!"

The story above is to make you aware of the true fight we are up against as men and brothers in Christ. When we walk into a new territory, there will come a time when we are tested. Evil will try to flex its muscle and inflict pain and destruction for being obedient to God. We must take our stand. We must honor that obedience no matter the price we have to pay. In every battle, there will be great men that will fall.

We must not stop fighting for each other so that we can honor the fallen, and those that still stand side by side with us in this fight.

I also tell you this story, to ask you to take a moment to honor a fallen brother. To pray for his wife as she heals! To pray for his daughter that she will know the man her father was in Christ, and that there will be many great Godly men that will walk with her in this life. To pray for all of his family to find peace in his decision to take his life. To pray for each and every man, those we know and those we do not, that God would bring an army alongside them to fight when they are too weak. I love you, Tim Peterson. I will miss you every day until I join you in Heaven. I will not stop fighting for every man, just as you never stopped loving and fighting for me.

There is a call now on each of us to build a bigger army of real authentic men. Brothers that will fight for each other in the Heavens through prayer, and on the earth through love. As we head to the last chapter, I call you brothers, not to run from this new battle. Not to run from this new territory, because you are needed! You are a vital soldier in the armies of God to help build His kingdom through your life and skills. Now, let's go learn how to build a bigger army together!

BATTLE PLAN CHAPTER 6

1. As you venture into new territory along your journey, who is it that you need to be helping? Who can you walk alongside and help that you either chose not to, or did not see before that needed your help?
2. What new territories have you been afraid to go into because you did not know the future? How can you walk into these new territories, obedient to God, not afraid of the unknown?
3. What blessings has God given you for your obedience in helping others fight for their kingdoms? How can you give God the honor in these blessings to keep your heart humble?
4. New Battles may bring heavy losses in our lives. To see God giving us a choice to continue to follow Him may be our greatest test of faith. As you help others fight, as you fight your new battles, how can you stand on the promise God gives us to keep expanding territory in His name?

PART FOUR

THE NARROW PATH TO GOD'S PROVISION

CHAPTER SEVEN

GOD'S ARMY, GOD'S GLORY

Let's start with probably the most important piece of this army, the Why! We, as men, cannot do life alone. We cannot fight battles of adultery, anger, fatherhood, marriage, lying, and depression alone. To grow and become who God has created each of us to be, we must do it together with like-minded men. Men who have come before us, who can show us how to avoid bad parts of their history, men who are in the same place as we are who walk lockstep with us in the fight of everyday life, and also men who are just starting in their faith journey, who will need your strength to teach them how to stand, and how to serve.

This is a crucial time for each of us because, as we have seen throughout our lives, the world will not do us any favors. The world will not just break and give us an easy life.

> **I applaud you for getting to this final chapter! It is not easy to look internally and choose to work on becoming a better man, a man who more closely mimics Christ.**

The pain and regret can hold us up from the future God has, and this is why we build an army. Therefore, we put the effort in to build a tribe around us. We can move more swiftly and make a bigger impact for generations to come by fighting alongside other men—more than we'll ever be able to do on our own.

A couple of weeks after Tim's passing, I picked up a book I had been reading, "Chase the Lion," by Mark Batterson. Opening the book to where I had left off was a section I believe God was waiting to show me until this very moment. It was titled "Pay the Price."

Here Mark spoke about defining moments in our dream journey. That when God gives you a vision and a dream for your life, there will be a cost associated with it. That we must pay to play! He then goes on to state God's promise to every one of us who are obedient to him, "Give, and it will be given to you. A good measure, pressed down, shaken together and running over, will be poured into your lap. For with the measure you use, it will be measured to you."[1] He ended that chapter with "Count the cost, pay the price, repeat as necessary!"[2] This was in terms of giving financially in his example. Here, at least for me, God was saying something a little different. It was not the money invested in Tim that mattered, but in being obedient to

God calling me to love as I have been loved. It was seeing that each measure we use will be paid back to us.

We have a responsibility, as I found out, to pay the price for the vision and direction God is asking us to go. For me, much like it will be for all of us, this price will come in the form of time, energy, humility, patience, and love. These are not just words here on earth, but I believe they are currency in heaven. God gives us these words as actionable weapons to fight battles and bricks to build His kingdom. We can learn a lot from our current military system on how to build these tribes. Let's walk through them and see how they relate to you and me in our quest to build a strong tribe that will contribute to the larger army.

RECRUITMENT

In the military, there is a starting process, recruitment. As I researched the recruitment process, I learned a great deal regarding how this is one of the most pivotal parts in building a strong army. Men and women come from all backgrounds and either choose to enlist or are recruited to join. The opportunity here to lay a great foundation of honesty, trust, and comradery is essential to the next stage of the recruit's journey. It is here we learn the macro view of the decisions we are making and how they will affect us down the road.

As a man, we must know what we are getting into. We must have a set of standards that we follow and would like others to follow as well. When this process in the military is done the right way, recruits understand the bigger picture of how the decision to enlist will impact their lives, the lives of those they serve, as well as what they will be doing for their country.

It lays the groundwork for purpose and direction. This resembles the acceptance of Jesus in our lives as Lord and Savior. We accept that we must become obedient to someone who is the Creator and Author of our lives. We don't understand everything that will entail, but we do know from the macro outlook that it will be blessed, and we will prosper because that is the promise of our Heavenly Father.

Throughout my life, there was always a calling for friendship, brotherhood, and leadership. I never knew exactly where that would come from, but I knew I needed it. I had fallen flat on my face too many times and knew there had to be a better way of doing life. As I fought hard in many battles, I became disheartened that I would never find a place to belong and find peace in the storm. This is much like the heart of many men today. Please know the army is coming for you. They are coming to walk alongside you to help you from this lone wolf walk.

Jesus gave us the greatest mission statement for each man when he said, "Therefore, go and make disciples of all nations, baptizing them in the name of the Father and of the Son and of the Holy Spirit." Matthew 28:19[3]

It is in these words that we can find a blueprint for recruiting others and enlisting ourselves into a new tribe. Through Jesus's example, He gave the disciples Vision, Time, and Compassion. These three pillars will require you to pay the price; that price is vulnerability. With that in mind, let's see how these three pillars work.

Vision

We know that God often came through visions in the Bible! This was one of the main ways He spoke to His people. Vision gives us the ability to see what is coming, to see what has not come, and use that to lead others. In

Proverbs 29:18, we are told: "Where there is no vision, the people perish." So, when we are recruiting other men to join our tribes, we must understand the vision God is asking us to cast for them. Can we convey the message of the gospel to them through not only our words, but how we live our lives? By knowing the man that you are enlisting and his Why, you can cast the vision of God's grace in his life. We do this by showing them what God has done for us. Vision is not lies and a fairytale ending to their pain and suffering. Vision is lighting the path for others to follow. Are you living in a manner that is lighting lamps for the feet of others to follow? Are you willing to humble yourself and let God's story through your life get all the glory, to recruit another man into this army of one?

Time

Eternal time and our concept of fleshly time are vastly different. While we cannot see all that God has done from beginning to end, we can see that He wants to spend time with us daily. As men of God, we must convene with Him daily to learn His heart. If we are doing this to the best of our ability, then we will understand its importance to another man. When you appreciate the time Jesus spends with you, you cannot help but well up and want to give it to another. In this humility, you will take the time necessary to walk along the new recruit's journey, as he discovers that he has the power to choose to enlist. This may come in the form of many phone calls dealing with issues, having coffee a couple of times a month to get to know the heart of that recruit, or maybe many invites to a Bible study where he does not show. This can be painful because you can see, as his recruiter, the benefits to enlist into this Godly army of men that fight for each other. But we must remember that our impatience does not glorify God's redemptive grace in our lives. Be patient with new recruits and give them the time that other men and God have given you. The rewards of this time have a greater impact on penetrating the walls of a hard heart than you can realize. God gives us time to learn and grow, let us do the same as we learn the hearts of the men we recruit.

Compassion

To serve a recruit, we must remember where we came from. We should always reflect on the great things other men and God have done in our lives![4] In turn, we must recruit through serving other men with compassion. Now, I am not saying let others take advantage of your time or your willingness to help them. What I am saying is Jesus humbly washed the feet of the disciples, and we should do the same. There comes a point in time in every man's life where someone stepped in and served us in a way we could not imagine. For me, it was Kyle. He loved and served me with his friendship and wisdom after my divorce. I thought we had lost our friendship forever. He put on the towel just as Jesus did and washed my feet![5] Figuratively, of course, but nonetheless, he made an impact through this compassion that made me want to fight for him, and a Godly life, more than I ever had. When someone needs help, we must see that and offer our service to them with no strings attached. By doing this, we will capture broken hearts that have been beaten by the world's dishonesty. Only by walking in another's shoes, will we have enough compassion to motivate us to walk along with new recruits in their journey to freedom in Christ.

When we put all three of these pillars together, we start to see the men gathering in our life. They come from different walks of life, just as the disciples were vastly different in personality and profession, to assemble together in a way that honors our Creator. With our tribe enlisted into service of Jesus and one another, we now must take our recruits and walk together into basic training.

BASIC TRAINING

"Hup, two, three, four! Hup, two, three, four!" That is the sound of the drill instructor as he is teaching the soldiers to march in time and in unison. When new recruits get to basic training, they must learn how to walk again. They must learn how to march to a specific cadence within a group, striving for the sound of one step amongst many people. The military does this because they must break new recruits of what they think they know. Drills as simple as marching together, sit-ups together in a row while holding a log, climbing up obstacles together, are all meant to harness the power of unity. Unity in mind and purpose.

While the military cut your hair so that you look like the man to your left and right, you all wear the same clothes and are taught respect as if you are an adolescent. There is a great reason for this structure in the military. They mean to break down your individuality so that you can harness the power of true teamwork. These tactics help recruits understand that no matter what they feel or are going through, they must contribute and work as a single unit to accomplish a goal.

While the men in our tribes are not going to cut our hair the same, at least none I have been a part of, we will try to create unity. The good news about God's army and basic training is that our unity comes through the gospel.

> We unify through the life, death, and resurrection of Jesus. With the Bible as our living drill instructor, we can hone our skills as a collective group.

What does this look like? Maybe it would be your tribe getting together for a weekly breakfast. Within that hour of time, you start to learn about each other, what makes each other tick, what pains or struggles is each man dealing with? Not only will this time be filled with manly banter and laughter, but it will also become a safe place to get better at doing life.

A great friend of mine described basic training as the "Crawl, Walk, Run" approach to life. This is a great mental picture of how we train each other to live better lives, through living together.

Crawling

In this phase of basic training, we learn to march together. This could also look like just being consistent for our tribe and getting together for breakfast every week, or having a group text, or doing a Bible study together. In the crawl phase, we are apprehensive about showing our whole hearts for fear of rejection. We want to belong, so we laugh and hang out and participate, yet we never fully engage. This is absolutely ok! Both vets and recruits need to understand first and foremost that this time in basic training together is a safe place—a place to fail, to heal, and to grow. The phase of crawling allows everyone to find common ground! Once everyone's feet get underneath them, it's time to start walking.

Walking

In this phase of training, we come to understand more of the hearts of the men we are walking with. We see humility, joy, and passion seep out in our time together. The walking phase may look like starting to have a conversation about issues such as pornography, politics, family issues, abuse, and even good things such as how God is working in your life. We learn to pray for each other in this walking phase, knowing it provides strength and protection for our fellow brothers. In my life, this has become such a vital phase because it has allowed me to truly get to know so many men in different states. This is where we can ask questions and get feedback. In our journey into this tribe, we must sharpen each other in this phase. We must test the morals and heart of each other. We do this to ensure that we are fighting for the same thing, unity and friendship. As we have started to march together as one, through consistency and honesty, it's time to start running.

Running

In this phase, the gloves come off. You and your tribe have been together for some time, sharpening each other, testing the waters of the heart! When you start running together as a unit, you see the momentum that is created through the obedience of purpose. This momentum comes in the form of one man texting the group on a Tuesday, saying he is struggling with lying to his wife. Your comrades come to support you through prayer and ask questions of why you're lying. They do not accept an "I don't know?" and press you, to be honest. As they continue to pray for you, speak truth into your life, and help you take responsibility for your actions, they do not judge you. They run with you! Great strength can be found in this harmony because a man's heart in failure will be devoured by the world if not protected by his brothers. We need other men to run at a pace that makes us keep up, keeps us accountable, and keeps us humble. It's in the running phase where blessings flow because God can use an army that will fight for each other, pray for each other, and give Him the Glory in the process.

The main point of basic training is to train. It's a place where you are continually with your tribe, learning, mastering skills, and picking each other up when you fall. This is particularly important because it is in the training that we form habits that will become second nature in Active Duty. Just as the military constantly gives you repetition and a task to become an efficient unit, we must do the same through our communication, love, and service to one another.

Take basic training seriously! The better you can become in this stage of building your army, the more powerful and efficient you will be when evil strikes. For over ten years, I have worked on this basic training with Kyle and Bryant. We live in 3 different states now and call each other on a regular basis. We talk about our lives, what we can use prayer and help with, and keep each other accountable. Our basic training has equipped us to handle life's obstacles together! We know that if there is ever a time when we are called up to active duty, we will respond to that call. We will do whatever is necessary to walk alongside each other to bring God glory and victory.

This is also a stage where you will see the fallout, so be prepared. In the training of life, we will have brothers come and go. Some will want to rise to the standard of the men around them, and some will not. Remember that both are ok because you are just called to love and let Jesus do the rest! Time will test your training and so will the world. This life will hand you an objective that may look impossible to defeat! Take courage in your training and the unit that fights by your side. The training complete, orders are in, we are headed out to Active Duty.

ACTIVE DUTY

We are here! All our training together as men, all the Bible studies, all of the sacrifices we have made to learn how to be brothers in Christ; your orders are in, to war! This war is for the kingdoms we currently rule over, for the future generations to come, and to stop in this generation curses that have plagued our families for far too long! You have been trained; you have a skill set that is important to the unit; now, it is time to use it!

This may come in the form of what I went through, for example. Over years of basic training with men in both Wisconsin and Florida, we were able to go to war when Tim passed. They were by my side, speaking life into me, letting me heal because of the wound in my heart, and lifting our families in prayer. It was like second nature because of our training to be the light God was asking us to be, to change the course of history! Though we have lost a great man, his family and daughter will have men to lean on when times get tough. They saw hope that there are men willing to walk alongside them in their worst moments when they themselves could not find hope!

You may have a friend battling cancer! It's time to deploy to that situation through unity in fasting, prayer, and helping the family in any way necessary.

Maybe it's your church that needs help. I genuinely believe they all need armies of men to stand up and fight when no one else can. Is your church always looking for volunteers to work events? Step up with your unit and serve quietly and humbly! Give God the glory and let the church see they have an army of servant leaders behind them.

This cuts deep because if we truly built better tribes of men in our own communities that were willing to go to war with and for each other, what would God truly be able to accomplish with those kinds of obedient men? Men that were created in His image, to be a light for this world, and to stop the bleeding of a fatherless nation! My brothers, as you read these final words, I pray that something in this book hits your heart harder than it ever has. May you run to the call God has placed in your hearts! This world, our communities, our families, and future generations need men that are willing to put aside how they feel and serve God based on obedience to Him, and sacrifices that bring him all the glory.

Crawl humbly with your hurting brothers as they need your compassion!

Walk faithfully in the Word as it will be your beacon and weapon!

Run towards the Roaring Lion as a single tribe unified in love and obedience!

May God protect you, brothers, as you journey through this life together! May generations to come appreciate the legacy we are trying to leave behind!

BATTLE PLAN CHAPTER 7

1. Do you have men in your life whom you can do battle with? If not, don't worry. There are more of us out there than you think that want to walk with you through life. Take some time and write down 3-4 names of men that you want or are doing life with. Let them know you're in this fight with them and want to become accountable to each other on another level.
2. Now that you see the importance of bringing other men into the fold, how can you reach out and help recruit even more men into the army of life? Can you start a group? Can you serve somewhere in your community? Find ways to enlist more men, as the more you have, the bigger the battles you can fight and win! (Be authentic, be brave, be a brother first to them.)
3. As you and your band of brothers go through life, remember the importance of crawl, walk, run. How can you as a group become more efficient together? How can you sharpen each other and hold each other more accountable every day? Remember, we cannot go blindly through life. We must train together to prepare for the battles ahead.
4. You have gone through a big realization, that you are stronger than you think, and you have the ability to learn and realign yourself to God's vision and purpose for you. The world needs more authentic men willing to fight for each other and our families. How, as a group, can you impact the community and your families? How can you, as a single unit, change the legacy for those in your kingdom? It's time for active duty, so go out and make an impact by letting God shine through you!

NOTES

Chapter 1
1. See Matthew 13:24-30, NIV.
2. See Philippians 4:19, NIV.
3. Marketingcharts.com/featured-105414, "The state of traditional TV: Q1 2020 Data".
4. See Genesis 1 & 2, NIV.

Chapter 2
1. Iron Man 2008, Produced by Marvel Studios and Distributed by Paramount Pictures, Directed by Jon Favreau.
2. Morgan Snyder, Becoming a King (W Publishing Group, 2020) Pg 38
3. See Acts 9:18, NIV
4. See Genesis 17:5 NIV

Chapter 3
1. See 1 Samuel 9:27 – 1 Samuel 10:1, NIV.
2. See 1 Samuel 10:17-25, NIV.
3. See 1 Samuel 13: 7-10, NIV.
4. See 1 Samuel 13:13-14, NIV.
5. Genesis 2:4 – Genisis 3:24, NIV.
6. See 1 Samuel 11 & 12, NIV.
7. See 1 Kings, NIV
8. Matthew 26:69-75, NIV.
9. 1 Samuel 13:14, NIV.
10. 1 Samuel 15:12, NIV.
11. 1 Samuel 15:28, NIV.
12. Jeremiah 29:11, NIV.
13. Matthew 7:7-12, NIV.

Chapter 4
1. Patrick Morley, How God Makes Men (Multnomah, 2013) Chp 3, pg 42.
2. See Jeremiah 1:5, NIV.
3. https://iowacorn.org/education/faqs
4. See Genesis 17 – Genesis 21, NIV.
5. Ecclesiastes 3:1-8, NIV.
6. Ecclesiastes 3:12-13, NIV.

Chapter 5
1. Luke 15:11-20, NIV.
2. https://www.explainthatstuff.com/bridges
3. Luke 12:51-53, NIV.
4. See Genesis 22, NIV.
5. See Psalms, NIV.
6. 1 Chronicles 1:1-12, NIV.
7. Exodus 12, NIV.
8. Nehemiah 3 & 4, NIV.
9. John 11:38-44, NIV.
10. Matthew 14:22-33, NIV.
11. John 13:1-17, NIV.
12. 2 Chronicles 1:11-12, NIV.
13. Exodus 20:1-17, NIV.
14. Romans 12:9-13, NIV.
15. Patrick Morley, How God Makes Men (Multnomah, 2013) Pg 38
16. Ephesians 6:10-18, NIV.

Chapter 6
1. Genesis 12:1-4, NIV.
2. Exodus 2:11-22, NIV.
3. Genesis 37 – 47, NIV.
4. 1 Samuel 17, NIV.
5. Judges 6-8, NIV.

Chapter 7
1. Luke 6:38, NIV.
2. Mark Batterson, Chase the Lion (Multnomah, 2016) pg 144-146.
3. Matthew 28:19, NIV.
4. 1 Samuel 12:24, NIV.
5. John 13:1-17, NIV.

ACKNOWLEDGMENTS

This book has been in the works for a very long time! There are so many people to thank, so let's get started. To my dad, mom, sister, and brother without our ups and downs and your never-ending love, these pages would not exist. To my late grandpa Bob for all of the wisdom and encouragement you poured into me for so many years! My Father, Andy, my best friend. Your example of tough love and always being there for me has forever changed who I have become! You have changed the legacy of our family and I am grateful to have such a great man as my father. May I love my family as much as you have loved us.

The beginning of my life, learning what to do and not to do, can only be attributed to my big brothers, Troy Gorton, Matt Bignell, and Keith Shultis. Thank you for treating me as an equal and toughening me up! To the men of ManCamp, I thank you for welcoming me in at a vulnerable part of my journey. It was here God and I found each other in a new capacity. You all have challenged me and loved me in a way that only Godly men can.

Griffin Gilstrap, my brother in arms in my new territory. Thank you for being a sounding board for this book as well as my passion to serve other men. You are truly blessed by God to see what others cannot and lead in a capacity that is unmatched by this world. Thank you for always seeing in me what I could not see myself and finding ways to bring that to the surface.

Kyle Weyrch and Bryant Renn, the men I run with, my sounding boards, my brothers! Each of you have walked into my life and have showed me what brotherly love looks like and what God requires it to look like. You have helped me stay humble, grow in my faith, and be accountable in a way I pray every man can be held accountable.

To my publishing company Two Penny Publishing and the whole team there. The excitement, knowledge, and belief you transferred to me in this process was incredible. I am forever grateful for your support in helping me bring a dream into the realm of reality! Tom Goodlet, your guidance and enthusiasm in this process has helped me in ways I cannot express. You and your team are making an impact and I am thankful to have had you publish these pages.

Last but not least my Heavenly Father and my beautiful wife Heather. God thank you for instilling your trust in me to write these words and steward this message with all you have put inside of me. Heather, I save you for last as without you I would not have had the courage and desire to carry out God's purpose for writing this message. May you always know how much I love you and am eternally grateful for you.

ABOUT THE AUTHOR

Dustan Christensen was born and raised as a hard-working farm boy from Wisconsin. After many sacrifices that left him empty, God opened his heart to restoration. His quest of not only aligning himself with our Creator but with other like-minded men has given him a passion and desire to help all men feel whole again. He strives to help men realign with God on what matters most and to build an army of warriors who can change their family's legacies for generations to come. Dustan is a husband to Heather, a father to Makenna Elyse, and a servant to our Father in Heaven.

www.ingramcontent.com/pod-product-compliance
Lightning Source LLC
Chambersburg PA
CBHW070809230426
43665CB00017B/2540